MW01439484

THE FULLER HILL KIDS
Catskill Mountains

Books By Deborah L. Gladwell
https://amazon.com/author/dgladwell

CHILDREN

The Adventures of Shy Spy Time Traveler-The Ten Plagues of Egypt and the Parting of the Red Sea

Mrs. Noah's Cat

Love Begins With J

ADULTS

Jesus and Things!-Poetry and Thoughts

Heaven and End Times

In The Beginning! The Mysteries of Creation

The Truth About Angels!

Faith With Jesus

THE FULLER HILL KIDS
Catskill Mountains

Deborah L. Gladwell

THE FULLER HILL KIDS
Copyright © 2023 by Deborah L. Gladwell. All rights reserved.

No part of this publication may be reproduced, stored in a retrieval system, or transmitted in any way by any means, electronic, mechanical, photocopy, recording, or otherwise, without the author's prior permission except as provided by USA copyright law.

Scripture quotations are taken from the Holy Bible, King James Version, Cambridge, 1769. Used by permission. All rights reserved.

This novel is a work of nonfiction. Names, descriptions, entities, and incidents included in the story are the truth, as seen through the author's childhood eyes. According to the law, the author has been granted necessary permissions for people mentioned by name in this book. Any resemblance to an actual person not listed by name is entirely coincidental.

Interior design by: Deborah L. Gladwell
Cover design by: Deborah L. Gladwell

Published in the United States of America

ISBN: 9798373969192

- Nonfiction > Biography & Autobiography > Historical
- Nonfiction > History > General

*In loving memory of
my Mother and Father
Joyce & Willard Thompson Jr*

To the best Husband in the world;
Kenny Gladwell
Sons; Kevin and Eric Gladwell
Daughter-in-law; Sara Phillips Gladwell
Sisters; Christine Taylor, Cindy Hulver,
Linda Shiflett, and Suzie Thompson
Love you all!

Special thanks to Kay Hampel and the
Colchester Historical Society, who have
cordially shared information and pictures.
I sincerely appreciate your help.

I would also like to thank my cousin
Ellen Finkle Ciferri, for the many
conversations regarding our ancestry and for
sharing family pictures with me. We are not
only cousins but soul sisters.

Prologue	1
Chapter One	8
Chapter Two	11
Chapter Three	18
Chapter Four	23
Chapter Five	29
Chapter Six	34
Chapter Seven	39
Chapter Eight	43
Chapter Nine	47
Chapter Ten	59
Summarized Genealogy - Pictures	64
Chapter Eleven	89
Chapter Twelve	94
Chapter Thirteen	103
Chapter Fourteen	107
Chapter Fifteen	113
Chapter Sixteen	121
Chapter Seventeen	136
Epilogue	144
Citations and Credits	149

Prologue

Fuller Hill is located just outside of Corbett, a small community nestled in the foothills of the Catskill Mountains of New York. The East Branch of the Delaware river flows along the edge of this tiny hamlet, adding to its homey feeling. Its crown jewel is the large [1]*Corbett-Roebling Suspension bridge built in 1926. Its suspension is said to be similar to that of the Brooklyn Bridge.*

This area of the State in the late 1950s and 1960s was known for its dairy farms and wholesome style of living. Most of the families of this era were not rich in monetary ways but were deeply rooted and bonded by family love. They would pass on their passion and values for generations.

I was very fortunate to have been part of this mountain life. I will never be ashamed of such a wonderful and blessed heritage. I may have been considered poor by many people's standards, but I was rich in ways most people will never experience.

My grandparents were Arnold and Florence Wayman Finkle. They were the parents of Donald, Joyce, and Florence. My parents were Joyce and Willard Thompson Jr. (Junior is what everyone called my father). I was the firstborn grandchild on both my mom's and dad's sides of the family. My mom said I was born on the hottest day of the year 1954. Since air conditioners were not commonly used back then, I can imagine it was a pretty miserable day to deliver a baby.

During my first months, I lived on Fuller Hill and was spoiled by my parents, grandparents, uncle, and aunt. In the days of my youth, I not only had loving parents but also coddling aunts, uncles, and grandparents that acted as parents to me. I never got away with much, but I'm sure my sisters will disagree with that statement.

A few months after my birth, my parents moved to the hamlet of Corbett. But when I became older, I spent all the time I could on Fuller Hill. Later my family would move many times to accommodate my dad's job, but we always considered Fuller Hill our central base, our home.

♦♦♦

Corbett is an old company town. [2] *The town's primary industry, from the late 1800s to 1934, was the Corbett and Stuart Acid Factory. It produced charcoal, ashes, wood alcohol, and wood acid. At one time, it was the largest acid factory of its kind in the world.*

[3] *The factory created many jobs for the community, requiring not only factory workers but also loggers and drivers. During World War I, the acid factory operated twenty-four hours a day to provide acetic acid, the main ingredient in smokeless gunpowder.*

The Charcoal side of this factory drew my Great Grandparents, Elmer A. Wayman, Elsie Coleman Wayman, and their family to move from The Slocum Hill, Pennsylvania area to Corbett. Elmer, his sons, and his daughter Sadie's husband, Fred Tuttle, and Fred's brothers all worked at the Corbett and Stuart Acid Factory.

The old factory was a mere shell of its glory days in the late fifties. Its walls had decayed, causing them to cave in. One chimney loomed majestically above the landscape. The others lay in disarray. The area around the mill had become tarnished with trash.

The old company store and post office were still open and thriving. Leonard Stuart, a descendant of the early owners of the acid factory and hamlet, owned it. Leonard inherited most of the houses in Corbett, including the house my parents rented in the hamlet of Corbett and my grandparents' farm on Fuller Hill.

Leonard was the kindest man. He loved everyone. I don't remember a time Leonard didn't give us or any child a few pennies to buy candy. Sometimes he would give us enough to buy a popsicle or fudgesicle.

The company store had wooden floors and shelves containing about anything a person might need. But, our favorite thing was a wooden framed penny candy display. I can tell you one thing it was always well stocked. When my sisters and I had a few pennies, we would spend forever peeking through the display's glass, trying to figure out what we wanted to buy.

◆◆◆

My mom and dad were very young when they married, and eleven months later, I was born. Meanwhile, my Grandmother Thompson died, and I was cheated of the opportunity to meet her.

Grandpa Thompson should have cared for his children, but he did not, causing his family to be separated. However, his daughter Jessie attempted to prevent this from happening. She strived to keep her younger siblings, but she was too young, and the State stepped in and took them from her. She married shortly after.

The younger boys were taken in by local farmers. The farmers took good care of them, but the boys were expected to work for their keep in return.

A loving Aunt from Tennessee, Aunt Mae Thompson, raised their youngest sister Betty. Mae was a widow with children of her own, but she and her family treated Betty as a daughter and a sister. Betty was well taken care of and very much loved.

As kids themselves and expecting their first child, Dad and Mom did not have the means to care for all of Dad's brothers and sisters. Unable to provide for his brothers and sisters always bothered my parents as they had such big loving hearts. Their house, however, was always open to family, and my parents welcomed them there anytime.

I remember when my dad's youngest brother Denny, developed bone cancer and came to live with us. I thought I would attend school with him when I was old enough to start kindergarten. I was so excited, but when they closed the door, and I saw him going down the hall, I began to cry. I was so heartbroken that I could not be with him.

School discipline was different back then, but it was also practical, and parents supported the teachers. My dad always warned me, "If you get sent to the principal's office, you will also get a whooping at home."

In the sixties, they did not have advanced technology, and my Uncle Denny passed away at the young age of seventeen. I did not realize, at the time, how bad his pain was. He tried to shield me from knowing because of my young age. I remember him screaming in agony toward the end of his life and me running next door to get a neighbor to give him a shot for his pain.

I still recall Uncle Denny's last day on earth. He was in the hospital with all his brothers, my parents, and my mom's parents around him. I wasn't allowed in the room, but he requested to see me. He made some small talk, told me he loved me, handed me a piece of gum, and told me to be good and go and play. He also entrusted me with his Bible, which I still have today. I only have good memories of my young uncle and pal.

◆◆◆

The Thompsons and Finkles had a strong work ethic instilled in them at very young ages. Later their hardships would help them to be understanding and generous adults as while as loving providers and parents.

Grandma Edna Mae Brown Thompson and Grandpa Willard Thompson had nine sons and two daughters. A set of twins and one son died as young infants. Life was hard for Grandma, who was often left alone to raise her children.

While in grade school in the Smoky Mountains, Dad and his brothers Thomas, Charlie, and Johnny picked coal up along the railroad tracks to heat their home. The boys also cut down trees with double-handled crosscut saws to provide firewood for winter heat and cooking on the old cookstove. They plowed a large field by hand so their mother could have a garden to feed her family. They always planted extra so their mom could preserve and give canned goods to their school. In return, the children were allowed to eat lunch there.

Two of the brothers were given an old mule and were so proud when they brought it home. They thought it would help them when plowing. However, the joke was on them because the mule was so old that it died that night, and they had to bury it the next day. The farmer indeed took advantage of some young boys and their mother. Their lives might sound harsh, but their experiences built character.

Farm life was not an easy life. Don, Joyce, and Florence also had to work hard, but they had a complete family unit to provide love and support. All three had various farm chores. Joyce recalls the three of them having to milk cows every morning and then rushing to the house to clean up before school started. Joyce and Florence also learned to cook, sew, and do housekeeping. These skills would later come in handy.

♦♦♦

This is a story of my life growing up in the Catskill Mountains during the late 1950s and the 1960s. This story takes place mainly in the location of my grandparents' home on Fuller Hill and my parent's home in Corbett, New York. I have found that one cannot talk of life without local history and current events, so I have also included them along with some local and family pictures.

I now have four sisters and four double first cousins, who are also Fuller Hill kids, however; we moved to West Virginia when my youngest sister, Suzie, was two. Due to their age, my grandparents moved to Downsville when Suzie was about five or six. This move deprived Suzie of adventurous memories on Fuller Hill. I also have many more cousins that I love very much but are not mentioned in this book.

We will start this story with my lifetime best friend and sister-in-crime, Christine (Chris). My dear sister, Cindy, was also present at the beginning of this story. She, however, was too young to participate in any adventures yet.

Chapter One

The town of Downsville and surrounding villages were in a flurry of activity as they prepared for the new Pepacton Reservoir project on the East Branch of the Delaware River. This dam and other Catskills reservoirs would provide New York City with ninety percent of its drinking water. Some were excited about this project and the revenue it would bring to its communities; others were against it as the reservoir would flood their farms, livelihoods, and communities.

[4] *Pepacton is short for the Lenape (Native Americans') word Peapackton, "marriage of the waters."*

It might have united the waters but separated many people from the land. Arnold Finkle, his wife Florence, and their three children, Don, Joyce, and Florence, were one of the families that were displaced by the Dam project. They were farmers in the small town of Pepacton, one of the towns the dam water would flood.

Most people never think of some of the sentimental things that such a monumental endeavor must change. Cemeteries were dug up, and bodies were moved to a newly designated cemetery on the back road by the dam. This was emotionally hard on the family members of the deceased. Also, family businesses and farms would be forever gone beneath the deep waters of the reservoir.

But even in the worst circumstances, good can be found. A fifteen-year-old man named Willard Thompson Jr. (known as Junior) moved to Downsville. His mom had many children, and life was tough for them. Junior sought work at the dam to help his mother to provide for her family. He was only fifteen but fibbed and said he was sixteen and was hired. On this job, he learned a trade that would later support him and his family, drilling and blasting rock.

Besides working on the reservoir, Junior also helped build the network of aqueducts that carried the water underground from Pepacton to its final destination of New York City.

Through his employment, Junior met a beautiful girl named Joyce Finkle. He fell head over heels in love with this sweet girl—thoughts of her filled his mind.

The Finkles moved to a farm on Fuller Hill. Junior often hitch-hiked from his family's Downsville apartment above a furniture store across the street from the Methodist Church and diagonally across from the old Pappas Soda Fountain to see Joyce on Fuller Hill. This was not a short walk; sometimes, he would not find a ride. But he never missed an opportunity to visit the love of his life, Joyce.

Junior often helped the Finkles with farm chores and making hay. He worked hard to impress his sweetheart, and a few days after his seventeenth birthday; he asked Joyce to marry him. The couple eloped on September 4, 1953, and eleven months later, I was born.

The newlyweds lived in Deposit and Newburgh, NY, after they married. While living in Newburgh, Junior traveled by ferry across the Hudson River to work. Shortly before my birth, they moved in with Joyce's parents and lived there until a few months after I was born. Then my parents found a house in Corbett to rent and raise their own family.

When Junior's oldest brother Thomas returned home from the Air Force. He stayed with the Finkle family and helped around the farm. Thus began a new love story as he fell in love with Joyce's younger sister, Florence.

Florence was a beautiful young lady possessing chestnut-colored hair, green eyes, and dimpled cheeks. Thomas was tall and handsome, with sandy-colored hair, blue eyes, and a wonderful smile. They were made for each other.

The young couple married and rented a house in Corbett. It thrilled Joyce and Junior that his brother and her sister married and settled in Corbett. They loved both of them dearly. When growing up, Joyce and her sister were very close to each other, and now they could raise their families together. It was a dream come true.

Chapter Two

My earliest memories of time spent on Fuller Hill are of Grandma rocking Chris and me on her lap as she sang soothing songs. We were indeed spoiled grandchildren.

Grandma had the prettiest long black hair; sometimes, she would let it down so we could comb it. It always felt like silk in our hands. Once when I was admiring her hair, she told me she was part Irqiqois Indian.

Another special treat we especially enjoyed was when she let us sit on her bed and go through her snap-bead necklaces. We loved popping them apart and putting them back together again.

◆◆◆

My sisters and I were also loved and blessed by the best parents in the world. Mom loved us with all her heart.

Money was tight, but Mom had the talent to make it stretch. She could sew or crochet anything from sight. She often used this talent to sew beautiful dresses for us girls.

Mom frequently read to us before bedtime. We loved the way she inflicted different voices and sounds to each of the various characters. It made the stories come alive in our minds.

Dad was a big loveable teddy bear and our protector. He always surrounded his children with love. My fondest memory of him is of my sisters Chris, Cindy, and I, crawling up on his lap and him telling tall tales of himself as a young boy. He often told stories of wrestling alligators and placing a stick in their mouths to keep them from biting.

My sisters and I truly believed his stories because he was so big and strong. We never tired of hearing about how brave he was. It never dawned on us that there was no way the tales could be true. Dad was from the Smokey Mountains, and alligators are not found in the Smokies. Our father, however, was not really lying, as he was the master of mountain storytelling.

◆◆◆

Time whizzed by, and I turned five years old. In September of 1959, it was time for me to attend my first day of kindergarten at Downsville Central School. I was so excited because I had watched Uncle Denny board the school bus last year, and now I could tag along with him and be a big girl. But what a shock I was about to receive. Downsville Central had classes from kindergarten through twelfth grade.

The bus unloaded, and Denny dutifully dropped me off at my kindergarten class. He proceeded to leave, and the door shut behind him. I knew there must be some mistake because I was supposed to be with him, not in a room full of strangers. I cried as I watched him go down the hall on his crutches. I begged him to come back between sobs. But, I received no sympathy from my teacher. She picked me up, whacked me on my tail-end, and told me to sit down and be quiet. I dutifully obeyed but was not one bit happy with my current situation.

I gradually adjusted to being separated from my uncle but was unprepared for mean classmates. Two girls who set behind me ruthlessly teased me every day, and when the teacher was not looking, they pulled my long hair. I feared getting in trouble or maybe even receiving another spanking, so I silently endured their cruel harassment.

Every morning the principal said a prayer over the loudspeaker along with the pledge of allegiance to the flag. We always quietly stood as he prayed. This was always followed by my classmates and me placing our hands over our hearts. Each child would face the flag hanging above the chalkboard and repeat the pledge of allegiance with him. When this was over, I would sit in my chair and hope the mean girls would be nice.

I enjoyed learning to print, nursery rhymes, and playing games. Music, art, and recess were fun, but I always cautiously avoided the mean girls.

♦♦♦

One thing that scared me was the **nuclear air raid drills** that were mandatory for schools. I didn't know what an atomic bomb was, but I knew it would kill many people. When the alarm went off, my class and the younger grade school classes would go to the basement and press our faces and bodies against the wall. Then the older grade school children would lean over us, shielding us further from a possible explosion. The high school kids came down to the first floor and lined up the same way along the hallway.

It always frightened me that if a bomb hit, what would happen to my family as they weren't in school? Where or how could they survive?

♦♦♦

Across from the company store in Corbett was a white building that used to be the **Corbett School**. My sisters and I attended Vacation Bible School during the summer there. It had a few rooms with wooden floors. Not only did we learn about Jesus, but we also played games. One of our favorite games was musical chairs. The snacks were always appreciated, too, as I had a big sweet tooth.

A Rummage Sale was held at the old Corbett school building that Fall. My sisters and I tagged behind our mother as she strolled through the many items for sale. Then suddenly, my mom stopped and asked me, "Look here, Debbie, isn't this a pretty dress?".

I immediately fell in love with the beautiful dress that was just my size. I was thrilled when my mom picked it up and placed it in her arms. I envisioned wearing the dress to school.

I couldn't wait to try on my new dress when we got home. It fit me perfectly, and I felt beautiful wearing it.

♦♦♦

The following Monday, I proudly wore my new dress, combed my hair, and ran gleefully to catch the bus. I knew the mean girls would love my dress and be nice to me.

I entered my classroom with newfound confidence, but this confidence was short-lived. When my two tormentors saw me, they started laughing and pointing their fingers at me. One snickered, "Isn't that your old dress?" The second girl smirked and said, "Yes, she's wearing the dress mom gave to be rummaged off to the poor people."

Never had I been so hurt. How dare these girls say I was poor!

That night when I arrived home, my mother asked, "Did everyone love your dress?"

I hung my head, and with a tear in my eye, I threw the dress into the trash. Then I brokenheartedly told my mother what happened at school. Then I stomped my foot and said, "I will never wear that dress again!"

Mom, with a sad heart, understood what I felt. She did not press me to take the dress out of the thrash. She knew these girls' mothers, and they had the same mean streak in school as their daughters. Mom, however, gave me some good advice, "Never let them know they hurt you. It drives bullies crazy, and they will leave you alone."

♦♦♦

Not everything was terrible for me during my kindergarten school year. One evening during supper, Mom and Dad announced that my sisters and I would soon be getting a baby brother or sister. Chris, Cindy, and I were so excited.

When it came time for our mother to have the baby, she and dad took us to stay with our grandparents. Before leaving, Dad asked his three sweet daughters if we wanted a baby sister or a baby brother. All three of us chirped unanimously, "A baby sister!". Bless Dad's heart; after having three daughters, he probably was disappointed that we wanted a baby sister.

After our parents left, Grandma heated some water on the cookstove, bathed her granddaughters, and put us to bed. We immediately snuggled under the covers and went to sleep.

The following day my sisters and I woke to the good news that we had a brand new sister named Linda. She was born one minute after midnight making her the first baby of the year. Chris, Cindy, and I were thrilled to have a new sister.

It was a big deal to be the first baby of the year. The local radio station made a 78 record of Linda's first cry, along with several songs (there was no such thing as a cell phone or a music app. back then). We were so proud to hear our new baby sister cry on the Walton Mountain Radio Station.

Life was grand, and now Dad had four daughters he loved dearly. His fourth bundle of joy came into this world on January 1, 1960.

♦♦♦

Soon kindergarten graduation came, and I was so relieved because I thought that meant no more school ever! After all, is that not what graduating means? I was very disappointed when I discovered that it was not the end of my schooling. However, on the bright side, I would have a few months to enjoy at home and on Fuller Hill.

Chapter Three

Summer was so much fun. I enjoyed the freedom of sleeping later in the mornings, and occasionally Mom took my sisters and me to the swimming pool behind my school. I played with my neighborhood friends and never felt sad as I often had at school. Life was grand.

Sometimes on hot summer days, Dad would get off work early and take us to a very special swimming hole. It was only about five minutes from our home up Campbell Brook. On this brook was a beautiful waterfall called **Corbett Falls**. It cascaded from a rock cliff and was like a small paradise to all the local people. Our unique swimming hole was at the foot of the waterfall. A spectacular hand-built stone wall covered the brook's bank along one edge of the pool of water.

The girls and I mostly played along the pool's edge because we could not swim. We loved it when Dad let us crawl on his back and swim into the deep water.

My sisters and I were told that the swimming hole contained giant catfish that could swallow little girls, so we never ventured into the deep water on our own.

Mom was afraid of water but always came along and kept a safe distance from the swimming hole. Dad and we girls, however, always playfully splashed her; she didn't seem to mind that too much.

◆◆◆

Sometimes Grandpa would drop by and pick Chris and me up to spend the night with him and grandma. We enjoyed these special times with our grandparents.

Other times, Mom, Dad, us girls, Thomas, Florence, and all their children would visit with Grandma and Grandpa. There was always so much laughter and good times up on Fuller Hill. In the evenings, the adults would play cards, or the men would retire to the living room to talk and enjoy the comradery of male company. The women didn't mind as they caught up on what was happening in the family and drank tea in the kitchen. My sisters and I loved it when we were allowed to sit and drink tea with them. It made us feel grown up.

On hot summer days, Grandpa would buy watermelon, and the men and kids would sit on the porch and spit watermelon seeds off the porch. Once, a seed grew into a watermelon in the space between the sidewalk and the porch.

When summer nights became hot and stuffy, the adults would sit in the rocking chairs on the porch. It was soothing to hear them laugh. We kids, unable to sit still, enjoyed playing tag or chasing lightning bugs in the yard.

♦♦♦

All good things must end, and so did summer vacation. It soon would be time to return to school. I was excited about shopping for school supplies and new dresses but did not look forward to another year of school. I dreaded even the thought of being bullied again by the mean girls.

I cringed on the first day of school when I saw my kindergarten bullies disbarking from their school bus. They never said a word, and I felt a feeling of intense relief wash over me. I was further elated to see that their desks were far from mine. I smiled to myself and thought, *This might not be so bad!*

First grade seemed to run smoothly until my teacher became angry when I could not grasp subtraction. My mom tried to help me understand, but she had a different method of doing subtraction than my teacher. This further confused me.

One day at school, my teacher lost her temper and took me by the hair, forcing me to look at the paper on my desk. With her teeth clenched, she growled at me in frustration, "Pay attention to what I am saying!". I felt slightly intimidated, but the teacher didn't seem to hold a grudge as the school year progressed.

Things seemed to be going okay at school, and I even enjoyed catching the bus at the Old Company Store in Corbett. When winter came, and the weather turned nasty, the other children and I gleefully played and threw snowballs at each other on the large concrete deck in front of the store.

On an icy cold day, I did something really crazy. Some kids dared me to stick my tongue on the metal rail by the store's steps. Not realizing what would happen, I did, and my tongue became glued to the rail. This really hurt, and I was in great distress. The other kids had no idea what to do.

When the bus arrived, one little boy ran to the driver to get help for his friend. Evidently, this was not the first time someone did this crazy stunt because the driver knew exactly what to do. He went into the store, got some water, and let it run over my tongue and the railing. Soon I was free but had a nasty sore tongue.

Sticking my tongue on the railing wasn't the only dumb thing I did that year. I had a good friend that lived in Corbett. It was about the same distance to my friend's house as it was to my bus stop. The only difference was my friend's bus went the back road to Downsville, and mine went the main highway to Downsville.

Mom would not let me change buses. I knew that my friend's bus usually beat my bus home. Knowing this, we devised a plan. We knew I could not leave my classroom without a permission slip from my mother, so I hid under my desk, sneaked out, and boarded the bus with my friend.

My friend's bus did not beat my bus on this particular day. Mom put two and two together and figured out what had happened.

When I disembarked from the bus, I saw mom and knew I was in trouble. Mom stood still, patiently waiting for me. She held a fly swatter in her hand, and I knew she wasn't afraid to use it. I was proven right when Mom applied the fly swatter to my disobedient backside as she guided me home.

Chapter Four

Once again, summer had arrived in all its glory. Life was good, and peace surrounded the Thompson household. Excitement filled the air when Grandpa and Grandma Finkle came to visit. We each fought over who was going to sit on their lap. We loved these visits because we had the best grandparents in the world.

When it came time for our grandparents to leave, Chris and I asked if we could go home with them. We jumped up and down joyfully when our mother said we could. Cindy, however, was still too young to join us. But this did not bother Cindy as she had Mom and Linda all to herself.

One of the perks of staying with our grandpa was he always had sweet treats at night. On this particular night, he had ginger snaps and milk which we both loved.

In the summer, everyone slept upstairs. Chris and I slept in a large bedroom we shared with our grandparents. The room contained two beds, one we slept in and one our grandparents slept in. The sheets always smelled like fresh air and flowers.

The brook ran along the stone foundation of the house. It projected a soothing sound as it flowed over the rocks between the foundation and the adjacent bank. A whippoorwill could be heard in the distance. The twinkling stars in the clear sky had a calming effect that lured us to sleep.

◆◆◆

I woke early to the comforting sound of the babbling brook. I peeked out the small window by the bed I shared with my sister and marveled at the sight of the sun peeking over the ridge behind the house and the little patches of fog that gave the field an eerie look. Birds were singing their early morning songs. A feeling of happiness filled my body. Then I heard the sound I was waiting for, the creaking of floor broads down the hall. Uncle Don was preparing to go fetch the cows to milk.

I excitedly shook Chris and whispered, "He's going to get the cows. Hurry, Chris, get dressed! Maybe, Don will let us go with him".

Chris and I dressed quickly and ran to meet Uncle Don. "Can we go with you?" we pleaded, never doubting that the answer would be anything but affirmative.

"Of course, you can go!" Don replied with a smile.

Don whistled for his dog, Maverick (which I also claimed as my dog). Then he called out "Coboss," "Coboss," which the cows recognized as come here, cow. Upon hearing this call, the cows obediently started moseying toward him as their bags were heavy with milk. Then Maverick jumped into action to keep them in line as he herded them to the barn for milking. He gently nipped at the heels of any cow that wandered off. Some of the more stubborn cows required an additional bark or two to show them who the boss was.

Chris and I rarely wore shoes in the summertime because it saved on the wear and tear of our shoes, and we loved the freedom of not wearing them. This freedom sometimes came at a cost when running in a pasture occupied by cows. For instance, stepping in cow dung and having it squeeze through one's toes was rather yucky, or stepping on a pasture thistle, thrusting its prickles into one's foot. This pain was not pleasant either. But as bright young girls, we learned to watch out for such obstacles.

The barn soon came into sight. I loved this old barn with its weathered boards. It had a silo on the side toward the road and a weather vane on the roof. I quickly glanced at it to see which way it showed the wind blowing today.

The cows were quickly guided into their stalls. There were two rows of stalls consisting of about fifteen stalls on one side and about ten on the other. The shorter row also contained a place for horses to be housed. Each stall had two vertical boards the cows stuck their heads in. When the cows were in position, the boards were pushed closed. The wooden panels were tight enough against their necks that they could not leave while being milked.

Both rows had small concrete ditches that ran behind the cows. These ditches served the purpose of cow toilets. Between the two rows was a small concrete drive. Later Don would drive a tractor with an attached manure spreader to clean out these ditches. He would then spread this dung mixture on the fields. It was excellent fertilizer.

Grandma was waiting inside the barn with her bucket in one hand and stool in the other, ready to join Don in the chore of milking.

Still too young to milk, Chris and I often chased stray cats throughout the barn. I remember once when, instead of playing, our grandmother taught Chris and me how to braid hair using a cow's tail as she milked.

Most people do not know that milk cows must be milked twice daily, once early in the morning and then again in the evening. Back then, it was not a job for wimps as all the work was done by hand and not by machines.

After Grandma and Don finished, they poured their milk into large milk cans and took them to the springhouse to place in a trough of cool spring water. This spring water ran through the trough day and night. The cool temperature of the running water kept the milk from spoiling. The cans would stay there until the milk truck came to pick them up and take them to the local Creamery.

♦♦♦

The Finkle home was what many call a simple New England Style farmhouse. It was a long plain two-story house that was two rooms in width and had no attic. It had a porch that ran the entire length of the house. This porch was built by Uncle Don with the flagstone that he and Grandpa cut from their quarry. It contained many rocking chairs, giving it a family-friendly and inviting appearance. The house itself was squeezed between Fuller Brook and a dirt road called Fuller Hill Road. This road divided the house from the barn and other farm buildings.

The Finkle kitchen wasn't anything fancy. It had a worn linoleum floor and open-faced white cabinets. The old white refrigerator was small compared to modern times, and its top was rounded. It had no freezer, only a place to freeze one tray of ice at a time.

In the corner was an old wringer washing machine that was used once a week. Grandma ran a hose from the spring-fed kitchen sink to the washer on wash days. After washing the clothes, she would run each piece through the wringer and empty the washer. She would refill the tub with clean water, rinse each washed piece, and run them through the wringer before hanging them out to dry.

In the middle of the kitchen was a huge round cherry table. Its legs stretched out from its center and looked like lion legs to Chris and me.

My sister and I anxiously watched as our grandma opened the woodshed door next to the cookstove and put a few sticks into the stove. We hoped that she was going to make our favorite breakfast, PANCAKES!

We were thrilled when she headed toward the old white and red Hoosier Cabinet and cranked out some flour from the sifter. Chris's and my mouths began to water as we realized our wish was coming true!

The old wood cookstove soon became hot enough for Grandma to place a cast iron griddle and frying pan on its top. She then commenced frying pancakes and eggs. She also put water in the teapot to make everyone a cup of tea.

Chris and I quickly joined Grandpa and Don at the table. Soon there was a large plate of pancakes in the middle of the table. Don grabbed a dish of home-churned butter from the refrigerator and placed it on the table.

Grandpa always poured bacon grease over his pancakes, but Chris and I never developed a liking for that. Don liked maple syrup, but Chris and I loved a delicacy that Grandma made, especially for us, *currant berry jelly*.

After breakfast, we helped with the dishes. Grandma had a big white porcelain sink. We carried our plates over and placed them in the dishwater pan. Next to the dishwater pan was another pan of clean water to rinse the dishes. Grandma washed the dishes, I rinsed and dried them with a towel, and Chris climbed up in a chair and put them away.

Chapter Five

The farm the Finkle's rented on Fuller Hill was so beautiful. It had two lakes that a hunting group owned, and it was Grandpa's job to ensure that no one hunted or fished on their land. He was deputized as a Special Deputy Sheriff, mainly for Fuller Hill.

Grandpa took great pride in his job. When he saw an out-of-state or suspicious-looking vehicle, he would jump in his jeep and head up the road to see what they were up to. Sometimes Grandpa made periodic trips to check things out. Often he would let Chris and me ride along. We did not really understand what he was doing, but we thought it was fun to ride with our grandpa.

Once in a while, Grandpa's instincts were right; he would catch someone that killed a deer. He would write them a ticket and call the local authorities to pick up the deer. Unknown to Chris and me, his job was dangerous because he was dealing with armed men. Thank goodness no one ever shot our grandpa or us.

◆◆◆

Tonight was a special occasion. My family was going to spend the night on Fuller Hill. Dad, Grandpa, and Don were going to fish for eel on the lower lake. This was necessary because eels ate fish, and they needed to be thinned out. The women folk were going to stay with Grandma, drink some tea and make donuts.

I never liked the sight of eels. They remind me of big fat slimy snakes. So, not being able to go eel fishing with my dad did not bother me one little bit.

After the men left, Mom and Grandma got the ingredients for making donuts. Grandma proceeded to get some grease hot on the stove. Then we girls cut out the donuts from mom's rolled-out dough and carefully dropped them into the hot oil. These donuts tasted better than any we had ever eaten. Maybe it was because we helped make them.

Meanwhile, the men boarded a small flat bottom boat and cast their lines into the water. Then they gently paddled the boat and drug the lines that held the worms behind them. A flashlight was used to light their way and to attract the eel.

Late that night, when the fishing trip was deemed successful, the trio returned and proceeded to clean up and process the eels for freezing. My sisters and I wanted nothing to do with this process and quickly left and prepared for bed without being told to do so.

♦♦♦

Chris, Cindy, Linda, and I were lazy the following morning and stayed in bed later than usual. We loved to look at the brightly colored quilts that Grandma made, which covered our bed. These quilts were all different. Some had teeny tiny squares, and some had beautiful designs. It was entertaining to see who could find the most blocks containing leftover material from ours or our cousins, favorite worn-out dresses. This was a game we were experts at because mom also made beautiful quilts from our dresses.

Downstairs, our mother began making breakfast, giving our grandmother a long-deserved break. Mom was a fantastic cook, but the girls and I often told her that Grandma was better. Maybe because Grandma catered to our likes. Mom did not have this luxury. Her favorite saying was, "If you don't eat what's on the table, there will be nothing else for you later."

The smell of the eggs and bacon frying and the aroma of toast grilling on the old cookstove finally lured us out of bed. Mom greeted my sisters and me with a gentle smile and seated us at the kitchen table. Once our tummies were full, we went to the living room to watch television. Grandma and Don returned to a fully cooked meal, and the adults sat down to peacefully enjoy their breakfast.

When Mom and Dad got ready to leave, Chris and I asked if we could stay with our grandparents for another night. We were surprised when our parents said we could stay, and so could Cindy. This was unusual but nice as Cindy was no longer a baby, and we enjoyed her company.

♦♦♦

Grandpa owned an old red 1930-something tractor that he plowed fields with and used to make hay. My sisters and I loved this old tractor and often sat on his lap as he drove it. Sometimes he would let us put our hands on the steering wheel as he turned it.

Earlier in the day, Grandpa had raked hay at a field further up the road, above Leonard Stuart's cabin. He had left the tractor in the field so it would be there when the hay was ready to harvest. He asked Grandma and us girls if we would like to ride up in his old truck and see if it was drying. We all happily jumped into the truck, looking forward to an adventure, and what an adventure it was.

The hay field was off the road and sat back in the woods. When our crew arrived, Grandpa jumped out to inspect the hay. That's when he noticed a red fox acting weird. Grandpa motioned for everyone to stay in the truck. He watchfully kept an eye on the fox as it ran in circles and continually fell over. Grandpa thought the fox might have rabies, a deadly disease for animals and humans. Not having his gun with him, he decided to go home and get it. He again warned everyone to stay in the truck and not to get out.

After Grandpa left on his tractor, the girls, Grandma, and I stayed in the truck. Shortly, Cindy became bored and rolled the truck window down. She and Chris bravely hung out the window and, without fear, tried calling the fox as one does a dog. The confused fox started creeping closer and closer, with foam dripping from its mouth. Grandma and I saved the day by grabbing the two daredevils and pulling them back into the truck. It wasn't long after rolling up the window that Grandpa arrived and put the poor fox out of its misery.

Chapter Six

Growing up, I was always blessed to have family nearby. Mom's sister, Florence, and Dad's brother, Thomas, lived diagonally across the street from us in Corbett. They had two boys (Tommy and Randy) and two girls (Edna and Mary). They are my double first cousins, and other than sisters or brothers, you cannot be any closer blood relatives. As cousins, we enjoyed many good times playing in both Corbett and up on Fuller Hill.

After summer hay was made on Fuller Hill and put in the large hayloft above the barn, Don would entertain all his nieces and nephews with a game of hide and seek. The hayloft took the whole upper floor of the barn and was divided by horizontal wooden dividers on both sides of the entrance. Tall wooden posts went from the floor to the roof. The hay was stacked almost to the ceiling as a lot of hay was required to feed milk cows during the winter months. These bales of hay made excellent hiding places.

Sometimes if the heat was sweltering, we kids would hide in the springhouse where the milk was kept. The springhouse temperature was always cool.

♦♦♦

Tommy and Randy, being boys, always had cap guns, and sometimes everyone played Cowboys and Indians. Other times we would just take a rock and hit the caps to make them pop.

All of us grandkids loved to play tag or dodgeball in our grandparent's front yard. This used to drive Grandpa crazy, as he was always afraid someone would get hurt. He didn't know that none of us were fearful of being hurt, and if we did get hurt, we loved how he would put salve on us and wrap our injuries up in torn sheets. Sometimes we looked like mummies, but we loved every moment of his pampering.

Grandpa had all kinds of salves. He had drawing salves and healing salves, and if there were any other types, he more than likely had them too. Once Chris and I got boils, Grandpa had a salve for that. Another time we got infected with impetigo sores, which he said came from being in the water during dog days, and he had a salve for that.

Our grandfather had a remedy for about anything. If any of his grandchildren got a bad cold, he would rub Vick on their chests and backs as well as on the bottom of their feet. Then he made them wear socks to bed, which we all hated. Years later, I read an article that Vick on the bottom of the feet was an old remedy that did work.

He would rub the juice from Touch-Me-Nots (Jewel Plant) for poison ivy. For diarrhea, he used blackberry roots. He was indeed a wise man.

♦♦♦

Tommy and Randy were the only boy grandchildren. Believe me, boys and girls do not think alike. Tommy was between Chris and Cindy in age. He actually was born one year from Chris and on her birthday. Randy was just eight months younger than Cindy.

Tommy loved to play a little rough sometimes. It wasn't that he was mean but just a young boy. He often kicked with his cowboy boots and was known to bite when mad. However, Chris had the cure. He bit her, and she closed a three-ring notebook on his ear. From that point on, Tommy played friendly, and he and Chris became best buddies. Tommy and Randy also stuck up for their sisters and cousins if someone else picked on them.

Chris was not afraid of bugs, worms, or snakes. She and Tommy loved to chase me with snakes because they knew I was petrified of these reptiles. Once, the two pranksters chased Grandma and me into Grandma's woodshed while holding a snake by its tail. Grandma clicked her tongue at them and said, "What makes you so?" It was amazing that poor ole grandma did not have a heart attack.

♦♦♦

My sisters, our cousins, and I liked playing in the dirt patch surrounding our tree swing. It was situated on my parent's property line and our neighbor's in Corbett. Many a time, we were warned about throwing dirt into the air. But we always threw caution to the wind and did it anyway.

One day while playing, Chris threw dirt into the air just as I looked up. My eyes became full of dirt, and I began to scream in pain. Chris ran to the house to get our mother. My parents dashed from the house, scooped me up, and took me to the doctor's office in Walton. When we arrived, a nurse met my family and directed them to sit me on a small table. Soon the doctor came in and ordered me to stop crying. Of course, I continued to cry in a state of panic and pain. The doctor, who had no bedside manner, squirted the eyedrop medicine he held directly into my mouth. This was unethical of him, but it did make me shut up as he worked on clearing my eyes.

♦♦♦

The dead-end road that both Thompson families lived on in Corbett ended at a patch of woods. Often during summer vacation, our mothers would pack us a lunch, and then we would go to the woods, climb up on some big flat rocks, and eat our lunches.

The woods usually had pretty violets or wildflowers, which we always picked for our mothers. Sometimes we would find orange newts and place them in small jars with lids. This always excited Chris and Tommy, but not me so much.

The woods always held terrific hiding places, and we kids loved playing hide-n-seek. Sometimes we hid too well, and the seeker would give up and call out, "alley alley oxen free."

At the end of the day, we all went home dirty but happy.

♦♦♦

There was one thing that I nor any of the kids in the neighborhood liked, ***Spring Tonic!*** It was the most awful-tasting stuff in the world. I remember several families getting together and lining up all the children, including me, to administer this gross medicine. Thankfully they eventually quit this spring ritual.

Chapter Seven

In the dining room of my grandparent's home was a huge walnut dining table. It was long and wide enough to fit my mom and dad, my sisters and me, Florence and Thomas, their four children, Grandma and Grandpa and Uncle Don, and more when company dropped by. Grandma and Grandpa always sat side by side at the head of the table.

The room also housed a beautiful walnut linen cabinet where our grandmother kept tablecloths, towels, and beautifully embroidered pillowcases. On top of this cabinet was a small sign that would forever be ingrained in our minds. "Don't lose your head to save a minute! You need your head; your brains are in it!"

Behind the table was a walnut china cabinet. It was elegant but did not hold fancy china and delicate glassware. However, it held things my sisters and I thought were beautiful, like the silver-leafed drinking glasses. These glasses were promotional items for laundry detergent. Customers would buy their product, and a glass would be inside the box. We also admired the ornate milk pitchers and plain dishes.

Almost every weekend, both Thompson families would have dinner with Grandma and Grandpa. It was a time of good food and company. Everyone loved this family fellowship time.

◆◆◆

Grandpa always reminded me of Santa Clause. He was average in height and hefty built. Grandpa also wore suspenders and always had a smile on his face. He had the most beautiful white hair and twinkling baby-blue eyes. In the winter, he always grew a mustache and beard, which clinched my vision of Santa.

The white hair and blue eyes must have been hereditary as all his brothers and sisters possessed blue eyes and, at that time, white hair.

Weekends were a special time of fellowship, especially when Grandpa's brothers Rease, Jim, and Aunt Laurie visited along with Little Jim and Frances. My sisters and I always called Little Jim: Uncle Jim and his wife, Aunt Frances; however, they were really cousins. Their daughter Ellen and I were cousins and close friends, as Ellen was about six months younger than me.

After dinner, the women would clean up the table and wash dishes. After they finished this chore, they sat and drank tea in the kitchen. They enjoyed conversations about their families and the projects they were working on.

The men would congregate in the living room and often participated in good-natured heated discussions. Of course, none of them were ever wrong. If an outsider had heard them, they would have thought a fight was about to burst out, but this was just their German temperament. They actually loved each other very deeply and always left on good terms.

While the grown-ups did their thing, we kids enjoyed running around and playing outside.

The following week everyone would load up and drive the short distance to the old Finkle Homestead in Andes and do the same at their house.

♦♦♦

The Finkle's often housed relatives in their time of need. They were not rich but lovingly shared what they had. I witnessed this many times. Once, my Great-Uncle on my grandmother's side lived with them. He was older than Grandma but able to help some with farm chores. While staying, he did not have to worry about bills or food because they took good care of him.

Farm families always had three full sit-down meals a day, and it was unheard of to have sandwiches. Often company would show up for dinner or supper. If there were too many for the kitchen table, everyone ate at the dining room table. On one such occasion, during the stay of my Great Uncle, a neighbor showed up at lunchtime and was invited to eat, making it necessary to have dinner in the dining room.

Chris was a daring child and a prankster. She snuck under the table and tied our great uncle's shoelaces together. It is still unknown today if he really didn't know that Chris tied his laces or if he just played along. But when he got up, he fell to the floor. Chris and I thought it was hilarious, but later we received a lecture on how dangerous doing something like that could be.

♦♦♦

Grandpa loved to tell jokes at the table. Every once in a while, our grandmother would click her tongue as she often did if annoyed. Then she would nudge him with her elbow and tell him to settle down. Sometimes one of us girls would tell some silly joke, trying our best to outdo him.

Being brought up in such a happy environment full of jokes and good times, it is no wonder that my sisters and I were gigglers. We usually thought everything was funny. Sometimes at the dinner table, we would get carried away, and our grandmother would tell us to stop. Of course, we never did.

Once during one of our giggling fits, my grandmother told us that someone she knew giggled at the dinner table and choked to death. For some odd reason, no one believed her. Thankfully, none of us girls ever choked to death, even when we laughed so hard that our ribs hurt and our eyes watered.

Chapter Eight

Most people have heard of the Boogie Man. I never met him, but I was petrified of him as a child. What mysterious powers he held, I did not know, but the mere mention of his name was very effective in keeping young children from going to or doing something unsafe. If his name was even whispered, it would stop me in my tracks as I imagined a sinister demon lurking in the shadows waiting to pounce on me.

One of the places that the Boogie Man supposedly lived was in my grandparents' cellar. The cellar was a dug-out room under the house. It was at the bottom of a steep set of steps that led off from the dining room. The brook that ran adjacent to the stone foundation of the house often seeped through the stones and into the cellar, keeping the temperature just right to place canned goods. It was always dark and spooky looking from the top of the stairs. The adults used this to their advantage because they feared that one of us kids would fall down the steps and get hurt, so they told us the Boogie Man would get us if we opened that door. Being gullible, we believed the adults. No one even questioned why the adults could go to the cellar and kids could not.

The adults did not mean any harm by using the fear tactic of the Boogie Man as a way to keep their children safe, but some kids, like me, became afraid of the dark. Sometimes I had nightmares of falling down the cellar stairs but would wake up before hitting the bottom.

One night I talked my mom and aunt into letting Chris, Cindy, Tommy, Randy, Edna, and myself, camp in my parent's backyard. We threw a sheet over the clothesline, gathered a few blankets and flashlights, and prepared for our campout.

The crew had fun until it became dark, and the lightning bugs came out. Everyone had seen lightning bugs before, but for some unknown reason, on this particular night, we thought they were the eyes of Boogie Men. We debated this matter back and forth and concluded that what we saw were not lightning bugs. Then we all screamed and ran to the house. It would be many years before we asked to camp out again.

◆◆◆

Drive-In-Movies were prominent during the years of my childhood. It was an affordable and enjoyable family time. Kids under twelve got in for free, which immensely helped large families. Cars back then were a little bigger, and more people could be squeezed into them. It was nothing for my mom, dad, my sisters, Grandma, Grandpa, Don, and I to pile in a car on a Saturday night and go to the Drive-In-Movies.

Mom usually popped popcorn, thickly covered with butter, to eat during the movie. She also made kool-aid to drink. We always arrived early to the Drive-In, giving my sisters and me time to play at the playground before the movie started.

Most of the movies we watched were westerns or comedies. But, one night, we watched a scary movie called "The Creeping Hand." Chris and I spent most of our time covering our eyes with our little hands or sneaking a peep between our fingers. This movie haunted us for a long time, causing Chris and me to check under the bed and our pillows before going to sleep. Fortunately, a solution to our nighttime fears would soon come in an unusual form.

The Walton Fair always fell on the week of my birthday. Grandma, Grandpa, and Don always took Chris and me to the fair for my birthday.

The night before our annual fair excursion, Chris and I sat still as our grandmother **curled our hair with rags**. Grandma took pieces of rags and placed a short piece of paper in the middle of it. The paper made the rag a little firmer. Then she took a small section of our hair and started rolling the makeshift roller. She brought up the ends when the hair was wrapped close to the head and tied them together.

The following morning she unrolled our hair and brushed it. We had the most beautiful curls in the world and couldn't wait to go to the fair so everyone could see our magnificent curls.

Grandpa always spent a lot of time looking at farm animals and horse races. This was always followed by letting Chris and I ride the carousel.

Sometimes my mom, dad, sisters, and I would go to the fair at night with my grandparents and Uncle Don. This was exciting because then we got to ride more rides.

One night Chris and I talked Don into riding the silver bullet. After a few times of the ride diving straight toward the ground, our uncle motioned for the attendant to stop the ride. He told the operator that we were sick, but he was the one that was ill. Poor man, he would do about anything for his nieces.

After Don recovered from the ride, he played a game and won a big yellow shaggy dog. That night when Chris and I were doing our regular bed inspection, Don came in with the shaggy dog. He placed it on the front side of the bed and said it would not let anything harm us. It was our guard dog. Uncle Don was correct; that was the end of "The Creeping Hand!".

Chapter Nine

Children had two types of education. Formal schooling was taught at a public school where they were expected to pay attention and to do well. The second was informal, and the children weren't even aware they were being taught. The second school was the school of life taught by their parents and grandparents. It never felt like school because it wasn't presented to children in the form of tests.

Chris and I, without realizing it, observed our mother and grandmother doing various tasks around their homes. Sometimes we would get in the way, but it never disturbed the older women. My sisters and I even had chores like picking up our toys and putting away clothes.

When Chris and I were old enough to sit still for longer than five minutes, our grandmother taught us something that would become useful when we grew up, sewing.

Quilting is artwork, and the person making the quilt is an artist. Grandma took great pride in designing every quilt she made. She always hand-sewed her quilts; she never used a sewing machine. It was relaxing and profitable as her hands were not idle, and her family's beds were never cold.

Chris and I watched as Grandma stuck a pin through a small paper square and a piece of material. Then she neatly cut squares until all the fabric was cut. The next step was threading a needle and sewing all the pieces together. This was time-consuming but worth it.

One day Chris and I said we wanted to sew. Our grandmother set aside her work and began our first lesson in making a potholder. She cut four pieces of squared material, two pieces for each of us. She waited patiently as we tried to thread our needles. When we finally accomplished the needle threading, she showed us how to knot the thread so it would not slide out of the material when sewing. Then she sat each of us on different sides of her and explained how the right sides of the material needed to face each other so that when they were turned right side out, the stitches would not show. She demonstrated how to hold the needle and stick it in and out of the material. Then she left us alone while we tried to master sewing.

After we finished three sides of our potholders, we ran to show Grandma. She turned them right side out and showed us how to stitch the top and put a hanger loop on them.

My first potholder would not have won any prizes, but I was proud of it. When Mom came to pick us up, we ran to show her our newfound talent. She praised us both, and we were so elated.

The next day Mom was mending some of Dad's shirts that had missing buttons. She and Grandma always kept boxes of buttons taken from worn-out clothes. Mom quickly found a button that matched one of the missing buttons. She then seated herself and called Chris and me to her side. Then she taught us how to sew a button on a garment. Chris and I found this new mending project exciting and proceeded to help Mom sew buttons. While we worked on mending, Mom told us how her mother used to make her **dresses from flour and feed sacks.**

Chris and I had often accompanied our grandpa when he picked up feed at Walton. The bags he bought were made of burlap. With this in mind, I grimaced at the thought of my mom wearing such a dress. "Oh, how awful, you must have been really poor. Didn't you itch?" I asked.

Confused by my outburst, Mom replied, "No, why would you think that?"

"Well, Mom, feedbags are made of burlap! Burlap is scratchy!" I stated matter of factually.

Mom laughed as she explained that flour and feedbags used to be made of pretty cotton prints. When she was young, people purchased the bags by the material they wanted to make a dress from or, if they were a boy, a shirt.

I was relieved to hear that my mother did not have to wear a scratchy burlap dress when she was young.

◆◆◆

Farmers always grew small gardens in the summer. The gardens provided fresh vegetables during the growing season. Farm families also canned many vegetables to eat during the winter months. Grandma was the master of canning. She canned anything she could get her hands on. Her cellar was always packed with vegetables, a variety of fruits, jellies, pickles, and meat.

Preparing food for winter is not an easy job. For instance, you must have berries to make berry jellies. Young mountain kids learn this lesson early in life. They know that berries don't appear washed and ready to be canned. Berries have to be picked.

I didn't mind picking huckleberries or strawberries too much, although I usually ate more than I put in the bucket. I loved blackberry and raspberry jelly but despised picking these berries because it was always hot outside at picking time, and they had thorns that put scratches on my arms. These annoying thorns made it almost impossible to reach the berries. I, however, loved a special treat that always followed berry picking: a bowlful of berries covered with milk and sugar. That made all the hard work worthwhile.

Apples were easy to harvest. Sometimes they required a slight bit of tree shaking, but Chris and I had no problem picking them up and placing them in the baskets.

Grandma stored some apples in the upstairs stairway to eat whole in the winter months. She peeled the others and made applesauce, apple curls, jelly, and pie filling. Chris and I were slow, but sometimes Grandma let us help peel the apples. We often made a game of seeing who could make the longest peeling chain.

When placing the apples in the stairway, our grandmother told us how they used to **bury apples** and dig them up later to eat.

"How did you find them, Grandma?" I asked.

"It was pretty easy," Grandma replied. "We dug a big hole, lined it with leaves. Then we put the apples in and covered them with leaves".

Her explanation made me giggle because, in my mind, I thought my grandmother meant that they dug individual holes and buried them. I imagined people aimlessly searching for hidden apples.

◆◆◆

It was a warm summer day, and Grandma had picked a basket of green beans. She placed her basket on the porch floor and sat down in her rocking chair to prepare them for canning. Chris and I quickly joined her. Our grandmother smiled and handed us a few green beans. She showed us how to take out the strings and snap the beans into small pieces.

Chris and I gleefully jumped into a rocker and began snapping beans. We felt we were big girls to be entrusted with such an important task. However, I probably ate more raw beans than I had snapped. I didn't really like them cooked, but I sure loved them raw.

We always enjoyed talking to our grandmother as we worked. Sometimes we learned interesting things. Today we learned that the old building our grandfather used as a pig pen and to store his jeep and farm tractor, amongst other things, was at one time the old **Fuller Brook Schoolhouse,** and as a child, Grandma attended school there. Chris and I both found this very interesting because we thought all schools were big and made of brick, like the one I attended in Downsville.

♦♦♦

Learning about the one-room Fuller Brook school was not the only historical thing we learned that summer. It was hay-making time, and Grandpa and Uncle Don had mowed and raked the hay in a field up a small dirt road leading off from the upper lake. Grandpa called it the Steele field.

When Grandpa got ready to go back to the field, Chris and I crawled up on the tractor and sat on his lap. Our grandfather told us this upper lake road led to an **old stagecoach turnpike.**

Chris and I had watched many western movies and knew precisely what a stagecoach was. Excitement surged through our bodies as we imagined Cowboys, Indians, and Stagecoach Robbers.

Chris asked Grandpa if he ever saw a stagecoach get robbed. He chuckled and said no, but he had driven many horse-drawn wagons. With a dreamy look, Grandpa told Chris and me that when he and our grandmother got married, he delivered feed for **Holmes Milling Company** out of Downsville, New York. He also said horses were all they had to plow the fields, make hay with, and travel back and forth to town or wherever they needed to go.

We knew our grandfather was born in 1901 but never thought of him, or anyone, working or traveling by horse and buggy. We only saw people with motor vehicles. Chris and I looked at each other, and I whispered, "Wow, Grandpa really is old!"

When our little crew returned home, Grandpa went to a drawer and pulled out a picture. He called us and held it out for Chris and me to see. It was a picture of Grandpa as a young man. He was in front of a big white building, sitting on top of a large farm wagon made from wood. It had rather tall sides to hold the feed, and his seat was perched on top of it in the front of the wagon. It was hitched to two big workhorses, one white and one black. The horses wore large collars around their necks. The wheels of the wagon looked like the ones we saw in western movies. In our minds, we could visualize wagons circling for an Indian attack.

◆◆◆

Although there was an A&P store in Downsville, the Thompsons, and Finkles did some shopping in the town of Walton. It was a little bit bigger of a town with a wider variety of items.

Going out of Downsville on the left side of the road was a beautiful waterfall. Grandpa saw Chris and me admiring the falls as we always did. Grandpa told us that the name of the falls was **Tub Mills Falls**. There were actually two waterfalls. The one above was not visible from the road. He said there was an old folklore about these falls.

> [5] *A family named Rose had a Tub Mill during the Revolutionary War. The mill was operated by the force of the waterfalls. They ground corn there, amongst other grains.*
>
> *It is said that the Mohawk Indians once surrounded the home of the Rose family while Mr. Rose was at the Mill. No one was killed because Mrs. Rose fed the Indians, however; they did take their milk cows and their son to herd the cows.*

Chris and I were amazed that, at one time, there had been Indians in Downsville. We couldn't wait to tell our sisters and cousins.

♦♦♦

In the winter Uncle Don would put little taps in maple trees and place buckets under the spouts. My sisters and I loved to go with him as he harvested the maple sap.

When he got enough sap, he built a fire and placed a big pot filled with sap over it. He then stirred the sap often until it boiled down to syrup. This process took hours.

Sometimes, Don would make maple candy from the sap. He went through the same process as he did for syrup, but he let it cook longer. When the sap started making foamy bubbles, Don would take it off, pour it into a flat pan, and let it cool. Then he would cut it into small pieces.

Don thought my sisters and I loved maple sugar candy, but we really didn't. It wasn't that we hated it, but we found it to be too sweet. However, we knew how hard he worked to make the candy for us and never had the heart to tell him we didn't like it.

While we watched Don work, he used the time as a teaching moment. He told us that the maple syrup process started with the Iroquois Indians. He said a chief threw a tomahawk at a maple tree. When the temperature rose that day, he noticed the sap running from the tree. He then tasted the sap and liked the taste. Later the Indians learn to burn brush to boil the sap into syrup.

When European settlers came and tasted their syrup, they found it very tasty. In those days, there weren't many sweets. So, led by their desire for sweets, it didn't take the settlers long to streamline the cooking process of maple syrup making.

♦♦♦

Sometimes our dad took the back road to Downsville. My

sisters and I loved this ride because we got to go over the **Downsville Covered Bridge**. The bridge crossed the East Branch of the Delaware River into Downsville. We loved to hear the car tires make clickety-click noises as they rolled over the wooden floor of the bridge.

The bridge was a single-vehicle bridge wholly made of wood with large wooden beams in the ceiling and huge timbered posts attached to the roof and wooden floor inside the bridge. Wood sheeting was vertically attached to the outside of the large timbers.

One day as we crossed the bridge, Cindy asked Dad if horses and buggies used to cross the bridge.

Dad laughed and told us that at the time of its construction, the main transportation was indeed horse and buggy.

Since his daughters had questions and he was familiar with construction, Dad gave us a little history lesson on the bridge. He told us that [6] *a Scottish immigrant named Robert Murray designed the bridge in 1854.*

My sisters and I were amazed that the bridge was built over one hundred years ago. We could visualize people dressed in coats with blankets covering their legs as they crossed the bridge in the cold New York winters.

◆◆◆

It was another beautiful summer day; my family, grandparents, and Uncle Don prepared for a long trip. Today my sisters and I would receive a different type of education. It would be an adventure of hands-on learning.

We girls were excited about this trip because we were going to the **Catskill Game Farm**.

It was very hot when we arrived at our destination, but that did not dampen our spirits. We jumped out of the vehicle and were ready to explore. However, before we could run off, Mom made each of us hold an adult's hand, and Dad carried Linda.

My sisters and I were thrilled when we saw animals we had never seen before. There were lions, tigers, elephants, giraffes, hippos, zebras, and rhinoceroses, just to name a few.

The big and dangerous animals were all kept in huge lots surrounded by concrete walls. At the top of the walls were chain-linked fences. This kept the animals in and allowed people to see them. It also protected both the animals and the people from harm.

Linda and Cindy particularly liked the petting zoo of baby goats, deer, and other small tame animals. While visiting here, a baby goat climbed up on a hay bale and tried to eat my hair. I giggled as I turned to see what was behind me.

All of us girls liked the small amusement rides. But we wanted to ride the miniature train that traveled throughout the park. We were sad when our parents said no. Being kids, we had no idea how expensive that ride was. However, we soon forgot about the train and ran to see the next animal. It was one of the most memorable days of our lives.

◆◆◆

The Catskill Game Farm closed on October 9, 2006, after being in business for seventy-three years.

Chapter Ten

Farm life had its perks, where else could one experience so much life? Grandpa loved to surprise his grandchildren with new animals. He enjoyed the expressions of wonder on our little faces when he brought home a unique animal.

Mom, Dad, my sisters, and I decided to surprise my grandparents and visit them. Shortly after we arrived, our grandfather told my sisters and me that he had a special surprise for us at the barn. We could hardly wait to see what Grandpa had brought home this time. Impatiently we pulled his hand to take us to the barn. He pretended he didn't want to go to the barn, but he really did.

Grandpa slid the barn door open and smiled as he watched his grandaughters gasp at the ram with wooly black hair and large circled horns. It was rather large built and had a regal stance. This magnificent specimen was given to Grandpa to repay a debt that someone owed him.

My sisters and I cautiously approached the ram; never had we seen one close-up before. We were careful not to allow it an opportunity to buck us with its horns as we lovingly petted it. Later we boasted of our experience to our friends.

Two critters that Grandpa brought home were loved by us girls at first, but later not so much. It was a pair of white geese. They were beautiful, and none of us could get over the size of their eggs. In fact, it was around Easter time that we gathered the first eggs and colored them. I even took a few decorated eggs to school for show and tell. The eggs were a big hit with my classmates.

It was later that these geese became aggressive. They often chased me, my sisters, and my cousins. All of us would flee from them with great fear in our hearts. These geese played dirty. When they bit someone, they twisted their head to inflict the ultimate amount of pain. Eventually, Grandpa had to get rid of the geese because they chased his grandchildren, other people, and even cars.

A little pony was my sisters, cousins, and my favorite of all the animals that Grandpa brought home. It was a friendly animal, and we were allowed to pet and feed it sugar cubes and carrots. The only drawback with this beautiful pony was that our grandfather was overprotective of his grandchildren. He always had Uncle Don saddle the pony, but none of us girls or our cousins were allowed to ride it alone. The only riding anyone was allowed to do was when Don led it around by its reins. At first, this was fun, but we all longed to ride the pony alone.

At one time, Grandpa had a workhorse. It was a huge bay-colored horse with white markings. It was stunning. Grandpa did use it some on the farm, but his grandchildren were never allowed around this gigantic horse.

Then there was the crow. Uncle Don caught a crow that had an injured wing. He and Grandpa put a splint on its wing and placed the crow into the old horse stall where they housed their chickens. They were trying to do a good deed, but when they took my sisters and me to see the crow, we gasped in horror.

The chickens wanted nothing to do with the crow and considered it an enemy to them. They pecked at it, further adding injury to the already hurt crow. Uncle Don immediately caught the crow and found an old rabbit cage to put it in until it healed and could be released.

The barn was also a place that stray cats always seemed to come to. When Grandma and Don milked, they always fed these strays. They kept the mice down in the barn and were rewarded with fresh milk.

The strays were often wild and unapproachable, but their kittens were not. It was a special treat to find baby kittens in the barn. My sisters and I always tamed them so we could hold and pet them. Sometimes our grandmother would let us take them to the house as pets.

My sisters and my all-time favorite pet was found on our grandparents' farm. Grandma had an old cocker spaniel which had been a pet since I was a baby. This dog had puppies in the woodshed, and we were allowed to care for them. We were ecstatic when our mom let us pick a puppy for a pet. We chose a black puppy with a white spot on its chest. She was such a beautiful puppy that resembled her mom. Whenever she saw us, she ran to us with her tail wagging.

Mom did not want a female dog but loved this little package of joy. She let my sisters and me name our new pet. We unanimously decided to call our puppy, Happy. It was such a fitting name.

Happy acted as a guard dog and followed us girls wherever we went. This made mom feel good knowing that Happy would not let anyone harm her children.

Being a dog, Happy also liked to hunt. Countless times she chased and was sprayed by a skunk. The smell was sicking and took days to dissipate. After being sprayed, I never understood why Happy repeated the same mistake.

One day when my family was visiting our grandparents on Fuller Hill, I saw Happy returning from one of her hunts. She was moving fast and making a beeline straight for me. When Happy stopped, I looked down and was appalled. Her nose was full of quills and looked like a pincushion. Happy had met her match with a porcupine.

Worried about Happy, I immediately ran to get the adults. Unfortunately, it was a lengthy, painful procedure to remove the quills. Porcupine quills are made to inflict the maximum pain possible onto their predators. The quills are hook-like at their end. This makes the victim concentrate on the pain inflicted on them and their inability to remove the quill. It was a hard lesson for the young dog, but it was one she did not repeat.

Deborah L. Gladwell

Summarized Genealogy - Pictures

Deborah Thompson Gladwell-08/13/1954-Walton, NY
    Husband: Kenneth D. Gladwell-11/28/1950-Bolair, WV
    Father: Everett Wesley Gladwell-Trout, WV
        12/9/1913 – 02/01/1988
    Mother: Olive M. F. Cogar-Helenda, MT
        02/06/1916-03/15/2006

Joyce Helen Finkle	**Willard Thompson Jr.**
Downsville, NY	Cumberland, KY
02/11/1936-12/01/2017	08/31/1936-07/14/2013
Arnold Donald Finkle	**Willard Bronson Thompson**
Andes, NY	Cherokee, NC
05/03/1901-01/04/1983	08/21/1909-04/14/1976
Wife: Florence Wayman	Wife: Edna Mae Brown
Slocum Hill, PA	Polk County, TN
11/20/1907-12/05/1985	05/12/1910-10/24/1953
Rease Finkle	**William Marion Thompson**
Andes, NY	Cherokee, NC
5/18/1864-12/09/1947	05/15/1882-05/27/1941
Wife: Elizabeth Liddle	Wife: Jesse Marrow
New York	Polk County TN
03/04/1873-1938	08/25/1887-05/17/1959
James Madison Finkle	**James Harris Thompson**
Andes, NY	Cherokee, NC
10/26/1835-11/11/1918	11/20/1851-12/02/1928
Wife: Helen McUmber	Wife: Martha Jane Rees
Andes, NY	Cherokee, NC
09/30/1842-01/01/1931	07/22/1852-1933
Adam Finkle	**Elisha F. Thompson**
Andes, NY	Cherokee, NC
08/28/1808-07/04/1874	1820-05/25/1911
Wife: Sarah Van Dusen	Wife: Amanda M. Grace
Nine Partners Patent, Dutchess	North Carolina
County NY	1817-Death Unknown
03/31/1810-02/18/1902	

THE FULLER HILL KIDS

Photo: Colchester Historical Society Collection, Colchester, N.Y.
Corbett and Staurt Acid Factory, 1915

Photo: K. D. Gladwell Photography
What is left of the *Corbett and Staurt Acid Factory*, 2019
Corbett, NY

Deborah L. Gladwell

Photo: Colchester Historical Society Collection, Colchester, NY
Corbett Houses and D&N Siderail, 1913

Photo: Colchester Historical Society Collection, Colchester, NY
Company Store

THE FULLER HILL KIDS

Photo: Colchester Historical Society Collection, Colchester, N.Y.
Corbett School, 1916

Photo: Colchester Historical Society Collection, Colchester, N.Y.
Corbett-Roebling Bridge Construction, 1930

As a child, I never paid much attention to the hand-built stone wall against one bank of Campbell Brook or the crevices in the brook bed above the Corbett Falls. When visiting in 2019, my son, Eric, pointed these out to me. I now believe that these two things might indicate that, at one time, there was either a water-powered sawmill or grist mill at this location.

◆◆◆

> [7,8] *Archibald Campbell was born in 1776 in Scotland and was a British soldier for five years before coming to America. He married Mary Jones of Wales, settled in Westchester County, and then on Brock Mountain, for a short time, before buying his property on Campbell Mountain. As one of the first settlers, the mountain he lived on was named after his family, Campbell Mountain.*
>
> *Archibald's third son, Archibald Campbell (born September 16, 1816), helped his dad clear the land when he was old enough. They built a sawmill and transported the timber down the river. When his dad returned to Scotland, the younger Archibald purchased part of his dad's estate and continued clearing the land and lumbering. He also raised stock and grain.*

◆◆◆

Historical records state that the Campbells had a sawmill but not the exact location it was built. Since they lived on Campbell Mountain and cleared land there, it is highly probable that they built one up Campbell Brook at Corbett Falls. We also know that the younger Campbell grew grain but are not told if he built a grist mill. The location of the sawmill was not documented, so we may never know if it was located at Corbett Falls.

Photo: K. D. Gladwell Photography
Corbett Falls – Campbell Brook, 2019
Corbett, NY

Photo: K. D. Gladwell Photography
Above Corbett Falls – Campbell Brook, 2019
Corbett, NY

Deborah L. Gladwell

Photo: Colchester Historical Society Collection, Colchester, NY
Tub Mills Falls – 1920
Lower Falls

THE FULLER HILL KIDS

Photo: Colchester Historical Society Collection, Colchester, NY
Upper Tub Mills Falls

Photo: Tub Mills-Upper Falls-2016-K. Parisi-Hampel

Deborah L. Gladwell

Downsville Covered Bridge
East Branch of the Delaware River
Downsville, NY

Photo: K. D. Gladwell Photography
East Branch of Delaware River - 2019
Downsville, NY

Photo: K. D. Gladwell Photography
Downsville Dam - Pepacton Reservoir, 2019
Downsville, NY

Photo: K. D. Gladwell Photography
Pepacton Reservoir, 2019

Deborah L. Gladwell

Photo: Colchester Historical Society Collection, Colchester, NY
Eagle Hotel Deer Season 1960s'
Downsville, NY

Arnold Finkle – Delivering for Holmes Milling Company out of
Downsville, NY

THE FULLER HILL KIDS

Photo by Junior Thompson – New York City, NY
Construction of the first World Trade Center
Destroyed by foreign terrorists in 2001
My Dad worked on this in the 1960s'

Road Construction – Dad's Drills    Road Construction
                                        Dad Loading a blasting hole

Deborah L. Gladwell

Cindy, Chris, Linda, Donny, Debbie, Tommy
Arnold and Florence Finkle's Home
Fuller Hill Rd. – Corbett, NY

Barn and Spring House/Milk House

THE FULLER HILL KIDS

Cindy, Debbie, Junior & Suzie, Joyce & Linda, Chris – Easter 1968
Old Fuller Brook Schoolhouse (upper right corner)

Florence and Arnold Finkle – Old Fuller Brook Schoolhouse

Deborah L. Gladwell

Grandma Florence and Grandpa Arnold Finkle – Workhorse - 1962

Linda Thompson, Grandpa Finkle,   Linda, Joyce, Junior, Chris,
Debbie Thompson   - 1962-   Cindy, Debbie Thompson

Grandpa was Special Deputy Sheriff for many years

THE FULLER HILL KIDS

K. D. Gladwell Photography
Upper Lake – Fuller Hill
Corbett, NY, 2019

Debbie, Chris, Cindy - 1960
How little girls used to dress
for Easter

Suzie
Hair set with Rag Curlers

Deborah L. Gladwell

Debbie Thompson on Fuller Hill

Joyce and Debbie Thompson
Appropriate pantsuit for
1969 school dress code

Grandma and Grandpa Finkle
Fuller Hill

Joyce Finkle Thompson
What we called a telephone in
the background (right of Mom)

Debbie, Chris & Suzie, Cindy, Linda

Back: Linda, Cindy, Chris
Front: Debbie Holding Suzie

THE FULLER HILL KIDS

Back Row: Grandpa & Grandma Finkle, Great Aunt Laurie Finkle, Joyce Thompson, Great Uncles Jim & Rease Finkle, Uncle Don Finkle
Front Row: Cindy, Linda, Chris, Debbie Thompson

Thomas & Tommy, Don & Grandpa, Linda. Lisa, Mary-Debbie-Randy, Cindy, Edie, Uncle Johnny, and Uncle Charlie

Deborah L. Gladwell

Florence Finkle, Joyce Finkle Thompson, Arnold Finkle

Thomas & Florence Thompson and family
Back: Randy, Tommy, Uncle Thomas, Aunt Florence, Enda
Front: Mary

THE FULLER HILL KIDS

Thompson – Easter 1968- Fuller Hill
Back: Debbie, baby Suzie, Chris, Cindy, Randy, Tommy, Mary, Linda, Edie, Lisa and John

Grandfather Arnold Finkle

Great Grandmother & Grandfather
Elizabeth "Liddle" & Rease Finkle
Holding Grandson Jim Finkle
Andes, New York

Deborah L. Gladwell

Right: Great-Grandmother Elizabeth "Liddle" Finkle   Left: Sister Ellen??

Great Great Grandmother Helen McUmber (Finkle Side)

Front row left: Great-Grandmother Jesse Marrow Thompson, others unknown

THE FULLER HILL KIDS

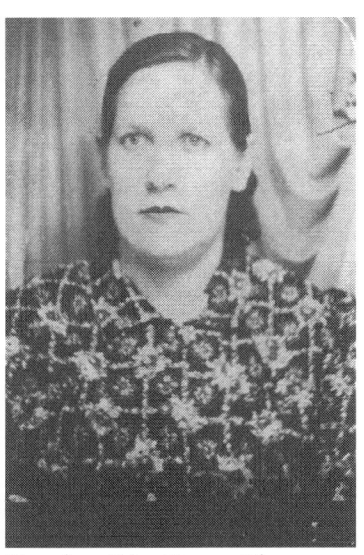

Grandma Edna Brown Thompson

Grandpa Willard B. Thompson

John, Junior, Charlie, Jeff Thompson 2002

Johnny trying to catch John,
Janice and Lisa Thompson

Junior, Jessie, Thomas, Charlie
Front Johnny Thompson

Deborah L. Gladwell

Jeff Thompson, 6 yrs

Back: Jessie (sister)
Front: Denny, Betty(sister), Johnny Thompson

Aunt(s) Sharon and Betty (Charlie's wife)

Dad's sister Aunt Betty Thompson Ramsey

Great Uncle & Aunt Lloyd & Mae Witherow Thompson

My Grandparents Arnold, Florence Wayman Finkle

Great Uncle & Aunt Fred, Sadie Wayman Tuttle

Great Aunt Grace Wayman Gardepe

ALL GROWN UP

Debbie Thompson Gladwell, Kenny Gladwell 1977

Debbie Thompson before wedding 1977

<u>Back</u>: Christine, Cindy, Linda <u>Front</u>: Debbie, Suzie

Deborah L. Gladwell

Kenny Gladwell-1968

Debbie Thompson Gladwell
1972

OUR SONS

Kevin Gladwell 2000

Eric Gladwell 2003

Chapter Eleven

Farming is not always a money-making profession. It requires long hours of labor with very little profit. However, most farmers will tell you they love their work.

Summer is a time for winter preparations. Grandpa and Uncle Don spent much time putting up hay for their livestock. Usually, they got two cuttings of hay. One in early summer and one in late summer.

Haying might seem easy to some, but it is backbreaking work. In the 1950s and 60s, a farmer cut the grass. He then tedded it to dry and raked it into rows before baling it with a farm tractor and baler. The bales back then were rectangular haybales that had to be picked up from the ground and stacked neatly on the back of a truck. Next, it was hauled and unloaded into the hayloft of the barn. It was bad enough that the haybales were heavy, but the sharp ends of the dry grass also made small scratches on one's skin, and the hayseeds seemed to always find their way under a person's clothing, causing them to itch in the scorching summer sun.

Chris, Cindy, and I were not big enough to help with the haying chore, but I knew I would not like it from my experience on the truck. A few times when moving a haybale, I encountered snakes. This kept me petrified and cautious.

Farmers had to be very careful when processing their hay. If it was put up too green or what they called wet and stacked in a barn, it would often get hot on the inside of the bales and burst into flames. The fire would then spread rapidly and burn their barns down. It seemed like every year, someone's barn burned down this way.

In the late fall and winter, after the grass dies down, the cows no longer have easy assess to food. This makes it necessary to subsidize their diet with hay.

In the front of the stalls in the barn ceiling is a small hatch door. It leads up into the hayloft. The loft holds all the hay harvested during the summer. Uncle Don climbs up into it each morning and evening to tear a few bales apart. He then throws the loose hay down the open hatch. After coming down, he takes a pitchfork and gives each cow some hay to eat while he and Grandma milk.

Cows were not the only staple food that the Finkles' had. Grandpa also raised pigs to provide meat for his family. My sisters, cousins and I loved it when Grandpa's pigs had piglets in the spring. They were so cute with their flat little snouts and curly tales. It was always fun taking slop up to feed them and to watch them nudge each other out of the way to eat.

Dad usually got a piglet from Grandpa for our family. He kept it in a building behind our house in Corbett. It always became a contest to see who could raise the largest pig, Grandpa or Dad. I can testify that scrap food never went to waste at either house. The pigs did indeed eat well.

◆◆◆

Many farmers had to subsidize their income to pay bills and purchase items. The Finkles were no different. Don often did carpentry work on the side. Grandpa, over the years, logged until he cut his leg badly with an axe.

Grandpa and Don were excellent stone cutters. They had a small quarry on the old dirt road above the lower lake. During one of my and Chris' stays, Grandpa asked if Grandma and us girls would like to go with him and Don to the quarry. Chris and I jumped up and down joyfully because we knew this would turn into a picnic.

Grandma hurriedly threw some food, desserts, and drinks into a box. Then our grandfather started up his farm tractor, and everyone else jumped on the trailer attached behind it.

When our happy crew arrived at the quarry, Grandpa and Don grabbed their chalk line, squares, chisels, and hammers. The first thing they did was decide what dimension they wanted to cut that day. Then they took the chalk line and square and laid out the cut.

Chris and I found it interesting to watch them hit their chisels with hammers along the chalk lines, causing the stone to crack. After that, they drove wider chisels into the rock until it separated and became a cut stone.

It didn't take Chris and me long to lose interest and begin to wander around and explore the woods. Sometimes we would find a fungus that grew on trees. We liked to carve our names on the big ones. Other times we would pick some flowers for our grandmother.

After the men finished their work and loaded the stones on the trailer, everyone again hopped on the trailer for the ride back home.

The next day Don and Grandpa loaded the cut stones on the back of their truck and took them to Downsville to sell. There was always a need for cut stones for various purposes, such as sidewalks, retaining walls, fences, and home construction. Grandpa always seemed to pick what was most in demand.

◆◆◆

Young boys were also taught early how to master farm chores. When Tommy and Randy stayed on Fuller Hill, Grandpa would take them around with him and Uncle Don as they worked. If they made hay, the boys were expected to do what they could to help. Sometimes it took both boys to lift a bale of hay until they matured and became more fit and able to lift one on their own.

The boys also learned the basics of stone cutting. Grandpa often rewarded them with a few dollars for their hard labor, but the boys enjoyed molasses cookies even if he didn't.

Another life skill that most boys learned was hunting and fishing. This gave them the ability to provide meat for their families.

Tommy and Randy especially liked to fish. This was something that the Finkle and Thompson men found to be beneficial and pleasurable.

My sisters and I often felt left out because we could not be part of these fishing expeditions, even though we did not like fishing worms or slimy bait.

Our father knew how his daughters felt and sometimes took us fishing. He made my sisters and me poles by taking little sticks and attaching fishing lines and hooks. Then we attached corn to our hooks and fished. Dad enjoyed the sight of his daughters' smiles when we caught a sunfish.

Dad never knew what kind of adventure he would have when he took his daughters and wife fishing. On one trip, he set our poles up, prepared his pole, and began to fish. Shortly, everything went sideways. We saw a watersnake swimming toward us in the lake. In a state of panic, we screamed and scattered away from the water, almost knocking our mother, who was afraid of the water, into the lake. Still clinging to her pole, Cindy caught her hook in the seat of Dad's pants as she whizzed by him.

Dad was very understanding and inwardly laughed. He must have been courageous because he still took his daughters fishing even after this incident.

Chapter Twelve

Most homes in the Corbett area during my childhood were two stories, as were mine and my grandparents' homes. The houses were not well insulated and had drafty single-pane glass windows. This made the heating of the homes expensive. To compensate for this problem, the Finkles and the Thompsons closed off their upstairs rooms during the winter. They also stretched plastic over the windows to keep down cold air drafts.

I thought it was beautiful when the windows frosted over. They looked like little individual snowflakes. My mother told me that Jack Frost painted them at night. She also gave him credit on frigid nights when the snow looked like sparkling diamonds. Ole Jack made quite an impression as an artist in my mind.

Our home was heated by one gas stove. This stove was in our living room to the left of the upstairs stairwell.

When my parents closed off the upstairs, they faced another dilemma; their home had no downstairs bedrooms. They remedied this problem by moving out the dining room furniture. Removing this furniture did not cause a problem because our kitchen was big and had a table and chairs. Next, they moved their bed, plus a bed for all four of us girls to share, into the dining room. Mom then divided the room from the living room by placing a long rod and curtain.

Our new bedroom was very cramped, but none of us girls minded because we loved being close to our parents. It made it more convenient to pile into their bed in the morning and wake them up. We loved doing this because Dad always made us laugh when he tickled us.

Being downstairs was also convenient at Christmas time as it gave us a sneak peek of what Santa had left before waking our parents.

♦♦♦

I was now in second grade and totally engrossed with everything to do with Christmas. The anticipation of Christmas day was almost more than I could stand. The joy of the season shone continually on my little face.

This year I loved my teacher, and the bullies were not in my class anymore. When I woke in the mornings, I looked forward to school.

My **school had a program** in which I had participated for a few years. One day a week, those who were part of this program were **walked to a church of their choice.**

There a class similar to Sunday school was held. This year they would also have a small Christmas service in which the kids would participate.

In school, we cut out Christmas trees from colored paper and glued decorations on them. Then the teacher displayed them on the windows of our classroom. The students also made a long colorful paper chain that the teacher hung on our class tree.

Once a week, our class went to an upstairs art class where the big kids were. I was especially looking forward to it today because we were going to make straw stars.

The library was also located upstairs. I always loved going there because the Librarian was so nice and read such beautiful stories. Lately, she had been reading Christmas stories which added to my excitement.

Second graders were allowed to check out books to take home. I chose "The Night Before Christmas." It made me feel big to read it to my sisters, and I enjoyed the beautiful pictures, also.

Chris was a kindergartener this year. Mom always gave Chris and me money to purchase milk in the afternoon. We both liked chocolate milk which was four cents. With Christmas coming up, Chris and I put our heads together and schemed a plan to buy a present for our mother and grandmother. A few months before Christmas, we hid our money and did not buy milk. Then when we went to the J. J. Newberry Five-and-Dime store in Walton, we purchased both Mom and Grandma a little green elf knickknack. We were so proud of our knickknacks and just knew our mother and grandmother would love them.

◆◆◆

A week before Christmas, Dad brought home a beautiful hemlock Christmas tree. He put it in a tree stand and added water to keep it from drying out and burning the house down.

Mom put a tree skirt around the bottom of the tree and got out all the boxes of Christmas ornaments. Mom always hung the colorful lights first. Their bulbs were rather big but oh so pretty. But she had to keep an eye on them when they were lit to ensure they didn't get too hot and catch the tree on fire.

After the lights were hung to our mother's satisfaction, the fun began. Each of us girls would pick out an ornament and place it on the tree. Dad and Mom took care of the higher places, and Dad put the star at the top of the tree.

Mom was kind of particular about how the silver icicles should be hung. She showed us every year how to take one at a time and drape it over a limb to make it look like real icicles. My sisters and I would start out obeying instructions, but soon we would revert to grabbing handfuls of icicles and hanging them in a bunch. It didn't matter to us because we thought it made the tree look beautiful. Mom would just shake her head and smile.

An advantage of living close to your grandparents is that one gets to decorate two trees.

Chris, Cindy, Linda, our cousins, and I loved to help Uncle Don get a tree. He always let us tag along and pick what tree we wanted, and then he would chop it down. One year he climbed a tree and cut the top out of it for us.

After dragging the tree home, everyone would decorate it. Our grandmother also had beautiful ornaments and silver icicles. She, however, wasn't too particular about how they were hung.

♦♦♦

My sisters and I were oblivious to our parents' finances. Dad was laid off early this particular year, and money was tight. They had four daughters and needed to buy us boots and coats. Being young and possessing big tender hearts, they wanted to give us a spectacular Christmas, which they did. However, no one knew Mom and Dad took a loan out to do this. Years later, Dad told me that taking a loan from a Savings and Loans Company, even though he loved making us happy, was a mistake because it was tough to pay back.

Santa always brought Christmas presents on Christmas Eve after we went to bed. He was pretty quiet because he never woke us up.

On Christmas morning, I woke first and peeked around the curtain divider. Never had I seen such a sight. The tree lights were brightly shining, and there were presents galore, but two tall walking dolls really caught my eye.

One had long braided auburn hair, and one had short curly sandy colored hair.

I elbowed my sisters, and all four of us pulled back the curtain and stared at the gifts. Then we jumped onto our parents' bed to wake them up to come and see what Santa had brought. Mom said to go back to sleep; it was too early, but dad edged her out of bed.

The walking dolls were for Chris and me. Cindy got a small doll and a Mickey Mouse projection camera. Linda received a jack in the box and cute little ducks that flapped their wings as she pulled them around the room. Excitedly, we littered the room with wrapping paper but were oblivious to the mess we had made and that our parents had no gifts for each other.

The toys were few, but my sisters and I loved them. We were also ecstatic over the much-needed clothing. We each got a coat, boots, hats, mittens, and pajamas. We also got underclothing that showed the day of the week on them.

We couldn't wait to wear our new coats and boots and go outside to play. But first, we had to participate in another family tradition of pancakes and eggs for breakfast. This didn't bother us because it was still dark out anyway. We each returned to the tree and played with our new toys.

After breakfast, my sisters and I ran outside to see what our cousins and friends got for Christmas. A few of the neighbors got new sleds, and they pulled all the kids around the yard. Tommy and Randy had received brand-new cap guns. Edna was a proud owner of a new doll, and Mary had gotten ducks just like Linda. They got other gifts too, but these were the ones they liked best. My cousins also proudly wore new warm coats, boots, and mittens, as did I.

Soon it was time for my family and my cousin's family to go up to Fuller Hill for a family feast. Grandma had a big turkey roasting in the wood cookstove and warm pies on the warmer above the stove. Mom and Florence got busy peeling potatoes. Mom took out the stuffing and made gravy when the turkey was done. She sure could make good gravy.

When Don was called to carve the turkey, everyone ran to take their place at the table. It wasn't that we were all that hungry, but we relished sitting at the table and enjoying the company of all our loved ones.

Christmas was indeed a memorable time of the year.

♦♦♦

On the night before Linda's birthday, everyone would stay up until midnight and play the record of her crying. Then we would sing Happy Birthday to her and wish each other Happy New Year before going to bed.

The Christmas tree was always taken down on New Year's Day. The silver icicles were not thrown away but neatly placed in their box. My sisters and I helped our mother take down the ornaments and carefully put them in a big box. Then Mom wrapped the lights neatly together to store away for next year.

Mom always placed a blanket on the floor to drag the tree out of the house. The purpose was to keep from getting pine needles everywhere, but it never worked out well.

I always felt sad after the Christmas decorations were taken down, but not much because it was Linda's birthday. Tonight we would have cake and ice cream to celebrate Linda's, Chris's, and Tommy's birthdays.

When you have big families whose birthdays are close, you only have one party for the family. This also went for Cindy and me, whose birthdays were a day apart in August.

◆◆◆

Easter was also a very special time of the year for our family. We always dressed up for Easter. I have a special memory of preparing for Easter when I was in kindergarten. Grandpa took Mom, my sisters, and me to a store that was going out of business in Oneonta. There he bought each of us a beautiful chiffon dress. Mine was blue because he said I was his little blue bird. Chris's was a pretty green pastel color and looked like a dress specially made for a little princess. For Cindy, he bought a spectacular pink dress with a spray of large pink flowers on its bodice. He bought a yellow dress for little Linda that looked so cute on her.

Easter outfits were not complete without pretty hats, little purses, and new shoes. So, after the dresses were selected, mom picked out hats, handbags, and shoes for us.

I was thrilled because I was now the proud owner of a pair of black patent leather shoes. They were shiny and had a buckle instead of shoelaces. I was in girl heaven.

Of course, we always colored Easter eggs which we loved to eat. It must have been the different colors on them that made them taste better. It was also exciting to wake up to an Easter basket full of chocolate that the Easter Bunny had left during the night.

♦♦♦

In the summer of 1962, prayer was no longer allowed in schools. Because of one person, all could no longer pray. Thank goodness our school still allowed its students to participate in the local church program once a week.

Chapter Thirteen

Uncle Johnny had joined the Navy and was on his way home to stay with our family during his leave. I remember eagerly watching for him from our front porch. Shortly I saw him walking up the street toward home. Everyone was looking at him as he walked. I thought to myself, *he looks so handsome in his blue navy uniform with its bell bottom pants and white sailor hat.*

When Johnny walked into the yard, I ran to meet him. He swung me high up in the air and hugged me before entering the house. Everyone was so happy to see him. Mom had a special dinner prepared, and after supper, Dad and Johnny sat and talked.

I always hated seeing my uncle leave, but he sent me a postcard from all the different countries his ship docked in when he was out to sea. I loved this and often dreamed of growing up and becoming a world-traveling sailor.

But for now, I proudly took his postcards with their funny-looking stamps to school for show and tell.

After Johnny had been in the Navy for a while, he purchased a Bonneville convertible car, and when he was home, he drove my sisters and me around town. Sometimes he drove way faster than he should have, but we thought it was fun. Then he would give us a nickel to go to the Old Company Store in Corbett and buy penny candy. Life was good.

♦♦♦

After Uncle Johnny left the navy, he moved to Durham, North Carolina. There he fell in love with Janice.

I remember being awestruck when Johnny brought Janice home to meet the family. She was the most stunningly beautiful woman we had ever seen, other than our mother. She looked like a movie star, her blond hair teased into a beehive bun and her make-up skillfully applied. Her southern accent added to her charm.

Not only was Janice beautiful, but she was also a genuinely kind woman. She didn't even mind when us girls plied for her attention. We especially loved it when she teased our hair and painted our fingernails. We felt beautiful.

Johnny and Janice were also fantastic dancers. They often entered and won dance competitions. I will never forget when Uncle Johnny taught my sisters and me to do the twist with a towel. He put on a Chubby Chase record, "Let's Do The Twist," and had us put the towel behind our backs with an end in each hand. Then he had us move back and forth and up and down, pretending to dry ourselves on the towel. Soon we were twisting like pros.

♦♦♦

Uncle Jeff joined the Marine Corps and also looked handsome in his uniform.

Labor Day was often a big picnic day for the Finkle and Thompson families. My sisters and I will never forget the one that Uncle Jeff attended dressed in his uniform because he had to leave from the picnic to return to his base. Our clan found tables close to the lake and laid out their food. Everyone was set to enjoy themselves as they usually did at the Bear Spring Mountain picnic area.

Mom, Dad, and our family, Thomas, Florence, and their family, Grandpa, Grandma, Uncle Don, Uncle Jeff, Great Uncle Jim, Great Aunt Laurie, and Great Uncle Rease were all there. It was going to be quite a feast.

All the women were excellent cooks, but Dad loved to mess with his wife and her mother. Every year he would grin and brag about how good Laurie's coconut cream pie was. It was indeed delicious, but so were Mom's and Grandma's. However, their facial expressions were comical when Dad bragged about Laurie's pie.

The lake had a special place to swim, but sometimes kids often slipped away undetected by their parents and into the water. On this particular day, that is precisely what happened.

Uncle Jeff heard a small boy shout for help near the dam area of the lake. This poor boy's head bobbed up out of the water and then back under again. Jeff ran along the small dam, took off his shoes, lunged into the lake, and swan out to the boy. Thankfully he was able to bring him safely back to shore.

Jeff was now faced with another problem. He was in his uniform when he jumped into the water and had to report for duty. This caused Jeff to be concerned that he would be in trouble. No one ever heard if he did, so we took it for granted that he must have made out ok.

♦♦♦

Uncle Jeff fell in love and brought Sharon home to meet the family. She was very pretty and shy. Grandpa liked to tease her just to make her face turn red. Sharon worked at the Walton Reporter; she was the first woman my sisters and I knew that held a job.

Sharon often let the girls and me sit on her lap as she showed us how to draw pictures that made things appear close or far away. Sharon also drew funny-looking V's in the sky that looked like birds flying. Sometimes she even colored in our coloring books with us.

All of us were happy with both our uncles' picks.

Chapter Fourteen

I never thought my family would ever live in any place other than Corbett; however, I received some disturbing news during the summer before my fourth-grade year. Unfortunately, this news would take us away from our Catskill Mountain home for two years. Our father had secured a job in Pittsfield, Massachusetts, working on a tunnel, and we would be moving there soon. At first, everyone was excited until we realized it was a long distance from our home and our grandparents.

Everyone adjusted fine to our new home. It had perks such as a museum with dinosaurs and fancy sound wave equipment. Pittsfield even had a live theater where my sisters and I watched Puss and Boots.

♦♦♦

A tragic event took place on November 22, 1963. President John F. Kennedy was assassinated in a parade in Dallas, Texas. He looked so happy waving to the people in his open-top car before the fatal shot.

My sisters and I became sad as we watched the horrific shooting of our President unfold on TV. We will never forget this tragic ordeal and the heartbreaking pictures of President Kennedy's little children dressed in their coats going to their dad's funeral.

♦♦♦

At Thanksgiving time, my family moved to East Hampton, Masseschuttes. Due to moving on Thanksgiving Day, our Thanksgiving dinner consisted of oatmeal that Mom cooked on a hot plate. This did not bother anyone; in fact, it was kind of fun. We were just happy that our family was together and our Father would no longer have to work away from home.

♦♦♦

Dad was working on a road construction job around Holyoke, Masseschuttes, when they uncovered dinosaur tracks. This discovery halted work until after the specialists came to observe the site.

We were so excited when Dad brought home two dinosaur tracks for us to see. One print was of a larger dinosaur, and the other was of a smaller one. For many years my sisters and I had the best show-and-tell exhibits until around 1968, when Dad donated them to a museum near Poughkeepsie, New York.

♦♦♦

Ed Sullivan was a show that my parents watched on Sunday nights. I remember the first time we saw the Beatles in 1964, on the Ed Sullivan show. The Beatles had been around for a few years, but it was the first the Thompson girls saw them.

My sisters and I thought John Lennon, Paul McCartney, George Harrison, and Ringo Starr were handsome. There was a bit of controversy about the length of their hair, but at this point in time, it really wasn't all that long. Who would have figured that they would go on to become the best-selling music act of all time?

♦♦♦

My fifth-grade school year was spent in Deep River, Connecticut. My family now lived in a third-floor apartment, which was a new experience for us. The apartment had a balcony overlooking a sidewalk and the main highway into town. I loved to sit and watch traffic from its high advantage point.

The only bad thing about our new home was the people in the apartment below us. They always complained that my sisters and I made too much noise and would bang on their ceiling. Then our mother would make us sit on the couch.

During our stay in East Hampton, I became a book lover. After we moved to Connecticut, I became a proud owner of a local library card and spent hours reading on the front balcony. In my mind, I could place myself in whatever story I read. My favorite book that I read over and over was Heidi.

◆◆◆

I always thought my mother was pretty, but I did not realize to what extent until my mother visited my school in Connecticut. Mom had a meeting with my teacher during recess time. I recall playing on the monkey bars when the other kids stopped and pointed toward my mother. I heard the awe in their voices when they whispered, "Whose mom is that? She is beautiful!".

I proudly boasted, "She's my mom!".

My mother was indeed beautiful on the inside as well as on the outside. She had a warm, loving heart and would often go without things she needed to give her daughters the things they needed.

Mom could fix anything around the house, including toasters or light fixtures. She filled her house with love and items she made by hand. Anyone that visited her home felt welcomed there.

Mom's interior beauty radiated and shone brightly through her outward appearance. She was a petite woman in stature. Her skin was flawless, and she possessed beautiful dark brown eyes. Mom also had long dark eyelashes and dark eyebrows that complimented her dark hair. Her serene smile was accented by two gorgeous dimpled cheeks. She had a natural beauty that required no makeup.

Dad was pretty good-looking himself. He had dark brown hair, a muscular body, mischievous grey eyes, and dimples, but what we loved most about him was his heart and love for his wife and daughters. There was nothing that our father would not do for us.

While living in Connecticut, I took dancing lessons at school. At the end of the course, the school had a Father-Daughter Dance. I was sad because I did not think my dad would miss work to come to the dance. My eyes lit up when he came strutting into my class. I was so proud of him and wanted everyone to know it. I merrily taught him the Cha Cha and Foxtrot, and I loved every minute of it.

♦♦♦

While living in Connecticut, Chris and I had to take a speech class. Our father was from the Smoky Mountains, and our mom was from the Catskill Mountains, which confused how we pronounced certain words.

During one of Chris' sessions, she told her teacher about how her father wrestled alligators and put sticks in their mouths to keep him from being bitten. The teacher was upset that our father told such stories and called him into the school to confront him. However, she had us read about the Abominable Snowman during class. No one knows what was said, but the teacher dropped her complaint.

◆◆◆

Deep River was close to the ocean. My sisters and I had never seen the ocean before and were in awe of it. It appeared to have no end. It was always windy and cold on the beach around the ocean there.

One day Dad informed Mom that he was going fishing and he and the girls would bring back supper. This thrilled us, and we hurriedly got ready to go with our father. Before leaving, Mom told us to grab a sweater because it was windy and cool.

Once we arrived at the beach, we girls played in the sand, and Dad went out on the dock with his big fishing pole, hoping to catch some fish. However, that day the fish were not biting. Dad finally gave up and called for us girls. Then he spied a fish stand. He swore us to secrecy and bought some fish to take home. We all thought it would be a fun trick to play on our mother.

Dad presented his wife with the fish. Behind him were his four giggling daughters waiting to see what their mom would say. Mom just smiled and never let on that she knew he hadn't caught them. The giveaway was the fish; our dad's fish never came home cleaned and wrapped in paper.

Chapter Fifteen

During our time away from Corbett, my family made bi-weekly visits to Fuller Hill. In the summer, Chris, me, and sometimes Cindy often spent two weeks at a time with our grandparents, which always led to us crying when we left to go home. It wasn't that we loved our grandparents any more than our parents, but we thought our grandparents were ancient and might die.

Grandma always told us that we worried too much and not to cross bridges before we got to them. She also comforted us by saying that she and our grandfather would live for a very long time.

On our way home, I would start writing my grandparents a letter, which would be done before we reached Margaretville.

Some of the roads over the mountains were pretty crooked, but my sisters and I liked crossing the Hudson

River on the Rip Van Winkle Bridge. It was named after the fairytale of *Rip Van Winkle*. The story goes that a man (Rip Van Winkle) fell asleep in the Catskill Mountains and did not wake up until twenty years later. This intrigued us, along with the size of the bridge.

◆◆◆

Above the old schoolhouse, on our grandparents' Fuller Hill farm, was a small grove of white birch trees surrounded by wild pink roses. The pasture surrounding them contained whitewashed rocks, adding to the roses' picturesque beauty.

The farmers of this time whitewashed rocks with lime. Grandpa said this procedure repelled insects that were bothersome to livestock.

During our two-week visits, Chris and I often liked to play house and clean out the nearly empty woodshed. We would make a makeshift table and use blocks of wood for seats. Our grandmother would supply us with a small embroidered tablecloth to put on our table.

When we swept the woodshed to our satisfaction, we took a little trip up to the rosebushes and picked some roses. We placed them in a canning jar filled with water when we returned. Then we stepped back and admired the beauty of our handiwork. We loved the aroma of sweet roses that filled our nostrils.

Sometimes, Chris and I would sit at our decorated table and play with our Barbie dolls for hours. We loved making dresses from our grandmother's scrap material.

The dresses we made were crude, but we thought they were beautiful.

◆◆◆

When Chris and I were not playing house in our make-believe home, we liked to feel like we were helping our grandmother. We often took her broom and swept her floor as we had seen our mother do at home. We especially liked to sweep the living room floor because it had something Chris and I had never seen before, *carpet*. It was a stunning burgundy color and made us feel like royalty.

The living room was a cozy room used to relax between chores and before bedtime, and it was also used to entertain guests. It ran the width of the house with two windows on the back side and a window and entrance door off the porch side. It also housed two bedroom entrances, and across from them was the dining room entrance.

The living room walls were made of thin narrow wood with plaster tape covering the cracks between the boards. It was painted a pretty blue-green color.

The furniture consisted of a couch, two chairs, and two rocking chairs. All the grandchildren loved to crawl up into their grandmother's lap and be cuddled while she rocked them in her rocking chair.

There was also a tiny black and white television that only received one tv station. Every once and a while, the wind would move the antenna, and the signal would be lost. Then Don would have to go out and turn the **antenna** until Grandpa hollered that the television was working again.

Grandpa liked to watch the news. He especially liked Walter Cronkite at six o'clock. All television stations went off the air at midnight (no twenty-four hours of tv back then). After it went off, Grandpa would go to bed.

Under a window on the back side of the living room stood an **old-time treadle sewing machine**. It was a piece of art all by itself. These sewing machines were not electric but were operated by pumping a large beautiful wrought iron peddle with one's feet. The cabinet was made of dark wood and contained three small drawers on each side. The wood also boasted a pretty carved ornated design. The sewing machine itself was black with a delicate gold design painted on it.

Between the television and sewing machine was a **party line telephone**. Back in those days, four families shared the same telephone line. If someone needed to make a call and someone else was on the phone, they would have to wait for them to finish. Often times people were known to be eavesdroppers and spread gossip about others.

The telephone system was considered high technology and a wonder. Its only function was to make calls (No such thing as games, facebook, etc.). To make a long-distance telephone call, a person had to go through an operator and was charged fees for making a long-distance call.

Grandma's sewing machine sat next to a **potbelly wood-burning stove** which Grandpa often kept way too hot in the winter.

♦♦♦

Sometimes when my sister and I stayed with our grandparents, the summer heat would be sweltering. It seemed to drain the energy from our bodies.

I believe air conditioning was around, but no one I knew had such a thing. To cool their homes, people opened windows, hoping for a breeze. This sometimes gave access for pesty black flies to enter. To counter the flies, people hung gooey fly strips from their ceilings. These strips captured many flies, but there always seemed to be more that escaped them. The gooey fly strips were also a nuisance if you were not paying attention and ran into one, thereby getting the yucky fly-covered strip in your hair or face.

Often Chris and I chased the annoying flies with fly swatters, especially when they bit. Grandma always said it was a sign of a storm coming when flies bite.

♦♦♦

Often our family spent the weekend on Fuller Hill. In the winter, Grandpa would put a bed in the living room for my sisters and me to sleep on. The only complaint we had, was that Grandpa kept the stove almost red hot and piled the covers on us. After he went to bed, we would kick off our blankets, but when he returned to put more wood in the stove, he made us cover back up. He thought we would catch pneumonia if we didn't stay covered.

Sometimes being uncomfortably hot, I would lie in bed awake. My grandparents had a clock that donged once for every hour and dinged once on the half hour. I found its steady ticking soothing and always knew what time it was.

One of the things we Thompson girls often got in trouble for was giggling. Most of the time, our dad ignored our giggles except when driving or trying to sleep. I recall once when my sisters and I were in our makeshift bed in our grandparents' living room. Dad was extra tired, and the girls and I were extra giggly. Dad warned us several times to be quiet and go to sleep. His warnings fell on deaf ears. Finally, in utter frustration, he entered the living room with his belt in hand. He flicked the strap across the bed, knowing it would put more fear in his daughters than harm because of the quilts. I was lying between my sisters, and his belt completely missed me. After he returned to his room, I snickered, "He missed me!" Hearing me brag, he returned and nipped me with his belt. I knew better than to brag again.

◆◆◆

One time our family visit fell on Easter. My three sisters and I eagerly went to bed early after coloring eggs. Our minds were on the chocolate bunnies that were always in our baskets.

The grown-ups could tell Cindy was faking and decided to go to bed and get up later. The problem was they were tired from their long trip from Connecticut and fell asleep. Therefore, they did not get up to put out the Easter stuff.

When my sisters and I woke, we were sad because we didn't see any baskets. Grandpa told us he thought the Easter Bunny might have left them in the barn by mistake. We all quickly dressed and ran to the barn, but the Easter Bunny hadn't left anything there either. Disappointed, we returned to the house, knowing the Easter Bunny had forgotten us.

We each entered the house with long sad faces and told our grandfather that the Easter Bunny had forgotten us. Grandpa smiled and said maybe the Easter Bunny hid our baskets.

We all cheered up and started looking around the house. Cindy was the first to find hers hidden behind the couch in the living room. Shortly, Chris found hers under Grandma's rocking chair. Dad helped Linda find hers under the sewing machine. I was beginning to think maybe I didn't have one when I spied mine under the dining room table.

♦♦♦

Sometimes during our stay with our grandparents, we would become bored with the adults. Then we would go to another room and entertain ourselves. Chris and I being older, liked to read or watch the television, but Linda loved dominoes. Often Chris, Cindy, and I would help her set them up. It was a painstakingly delicate procedure to sit them in the correct position, but the joy on Linda's face when she took her little finger and touched the first domino made it all worthwhile. She always got so excited as she watched each domino fall. We would never admit it, but we also enjoyed watching them fall.

Chapter Sixteen

The school year was over, and my sisters and I joyfully howled, "School's out, school's out, the teacher let the monkeys out!" as we skipped home. When we burst into our apartment, we noticed our father was home and grinning from ear to ear. He preceded to tell us we were moving to Downsville, New York.

My sisters and I jumped up and down in joy. We could hardly wait to be that close to our grandparents and Don again. Also, Thomas' family lived in an apartment over the A & P Store in Downsville, and our aunts, uncles, and cousins on both sides of the family would be close by. Oh, Happy Day!

♦♦♦

It's funny how life has circled; Dad and Mom found a house to rent along the Pepacton Reservoir. The very thing that brought them together in the beginning. Now the couple would be living there with their daughters. Life sure was good.

The house sat on a hill overlooking the reservoir. The trees along the reservoir banks were still short from being cut down during its construction. This gave our family a birds-eye view of the beautiful body of water. It was a magnificent sight that none of us ever tired of. The low tree line also allowed us to see the road that circled the reservoir for miles. This was handy when we sat in the bay window, watching for our grandparents' vehicle.

The house was a large elegant house with a small front porch trimmed with fancy lattice railings. Hanging from the porch roof was a crystal windchime. When the wind blew, it made the prettiest music I had ever heard.

Our new home also had a garage in the basement to park Dad's car. A small set of stairs went from the garage to the kitchen. The basement also had a place for can goods and a dark room for potatoes and onions.

The first floor had a beautiful wood floor in the living room and a linoleum floor in the kitchen. The bay window was located in the living room and had a special chair placed there. I loved to stare out this window when it rained.

One thing my sisters and I liked the most about this house was its enormous bathroom. We loved to bathe in the big white porcelain-clawed-foot tub. The bathtub itself wasn't any different than any other bathtub of the time. It just seemed more luxurious in this large bathroom.

The upstairs was very charming and had enough rooms to allow me my own room. My bedroom had a big bed and fancy furniture. I especially liked the dressing table that I sometimes used as a desk. I loved to write my thoughts and daydreams in a diary I received for Christmas, then lock the diary and put it on my desk.

Sometimes in my private sanctuary, I would read for hours or dream of growing up, falling in love with a handsome man, and getting married.

Another thing the girls and I liked to do was look through the Montgomery Ward Christmas Wishbook. It was a catalog with all kinds of beautiful dresses, shoes, and, best of all, "toys." We all took pleasure in imagining what Santa might bring us for Christmas.

The property also had a ranch-style house that no one occupied. This gave our family the privacy we hadn't experienced in a long time. We could run and play without neighbors being upset. Dad even bought us a game called croquet to play in the yard. Often when company came, the adults played it, also. No one could complain about the noise.

The girls, our mother, and I often walked to a field next to the house. This field contained blackberry and raspberry bushes galore. The bushes were tamed and lined in a row, so they didn't scratch the skin very much.

Mom made yummy jelly from the berries she and we girls picked that summer.

Our dog, Happy, could run freely again, but she still had the bad habit of chasing skunks. She was a prime example of the saying, "You can't teach old dogs new tricks."

♦♦♦

Sometimes in the evenings, our father would load our family into his car, and we would visit relatives in Andes. Traveling in the dark made the journey seem longer for the girls and me.

On these road trips, our parents loved listening to the music of the Wheeling Jamboree's Radio Station out of Wheeling, West Virginia. They could only pick it up on Saturday night on the road to Andes. None of the family knew that fate would move us to West Virginia years later, and I would even go to college in Wheeling.

♦♦♦

One night while living above the reservoir, my cousin and friend Ellen, her two brothers, and her parents came to visit. Ellen and I begged our parents to let me go home with her and spend the night. Both sets of parents tried to tell us that if I got homesick, I had to stay and couldn't come home. I remember boasting, "I stay at Grandma's all the time. I will be okay".

When we arrived at Ellen's house, all went smoothly until bedtime, and we began to tell ghost stories. Ellen added a little twist by telling me that their house was haunted. It wasn't long before I wanted to go home, but I knew I couldn't. It was a long night, but the next day was a blast.

Mid-morning, Ellen and I went to the General Store not far from her house. It was scalding hot out, and we each purchased an ice cream bar to eat on our journey to the School that Ellen attended. We swang on the swings for a while, then sat on a bench and talked. I was happy that I had stayed.

♦♦♦

Mom and Dad were still a very young couple with four children. They had rented but never owned a home of their own. Mom's cousin, Clark Tuttle, and his wife, Marge, had bought a house and had a house trailer for sale. It was small but affordable, so my parents bought it. They were also able to make a deal to leave it parked where it was for a small rental fee.

Our family moved into our new home in the village of Downsville. My sisters and I were intrigued that our new home was not far from the Tub Mills Falls that Chris and I so admired

Things were pretty cramped in our small home, but everyone loved it. We girls all shared one bedroom, but we didn't mind. The problem of our tiny bedroom was solved by bunk beds. Chris and I wasted no time in claiming the top beds.

The living quarters were probably more inconvenient for our parents than for us girls. No one could go to the bathroom unless they passed through our parent's bedroom. The bathroom had two sets of sliding doors, one on each side of the room. My sisters and I had to pass through our parents' room and the bathroom to get to our bedroom.

Our bedroom had a few overhead cabinets in which we stored our toys. It also had one little closet and dresser. This was not a problem because we didn't have many clothes anyway. But my sisters and I counted ourselves blessed because our mother always ensured that we were appropriately dressed in clean and ironed dresses, but we had no extras.

No one ever threw clothing or shoes away. They were handed down from one child to another. After the last in the family outgrew them, the clothing was bagged up and given to another relative. It was like a mini Christmas to go through the bags to see if anything fit you. The other families felt the same way.

Mom and Dad bought a small house on Knox Avenue the following spring. They didn't buy it for the home but for the land to move our trailer onto. Dad told me something I would never forget, "Land is the best investment anyone can make; it only goes up in value."

That spring, my family moved to our new property and rented the house to Johnny and Janice and later to Dad's brother Charlie and his wife, Betty.

Uncle Charlie and Aunt Betty were both quiet people. Charlie was always kind to me and had a good sense of humor. Often all dad's brothers would get together and play cards at their house on the backside of the river in Downsville.

Betty was a beautiful woman with a true heart-shaped face. Her complexion was pale and accented by her beautiful auburn hair. She possessed a sweet smile and was a soft-spoken woman. Betty also had a heart condition, but few people knew that.

♦♦♦

It was once again time to prepare for a new year of school. I felt excited because my class would be the first to have lessons outside the school in trailers. Our special classrooms were necessary due to overcrowding in the school. The overcrowding was caused by what the school officials called baby boomers. This term referred to the large influx of babies born after World War II until 1964. However, after the Korean War ended in 1953, there was a slightly more significant uptick in births.

I, although excited, was also a little anxious about how I would fit in after being away for two years. When I entered my class, the first thing I saw was the two mean girls. A feeling of Deja Vu washed over me. But, to my amazement, they were no longer bullies. They greeted me with friendly smiles, which immediately put me to ease.

Living in town had its perks. Because the girls and I walked to school, we could participate in after-school activities. This was nice because this year, the Junior High of Downsville Central School was letting sixth-grade girls try out for majorettes. The girls chosen would train with the older majorettes and even be allowed to march in parades. I was amazed that I was picked along with three other sixth graders.

I practiced outside our trailer daily, in the rain, snow, or fair weather. Then came the big day of the Memorial Day Parade. The sixth-grade majorettes wore white peddle pushers, black sleeveless turtle-necked shirts, and white tennis shoes. I was proud to be a part of this parade. My family was proud of me also and cheered me on from the parade's sidelines.

The parade always ended at the Paige Cemetery. My family met me there, and we all went up to pay respect and place flowers on the graves of Grandma Thompson, Uncle Denny, and Great-Uncle Lloyd Thompson.

♦♦♦

Heavy snows were not uncommon in the Catskills. Sometimes it was a little hairy getting around, but people always managed. The schools were rarely closed because of snow or cold weather. You were excused if you could not make it, but class continued.

Fuller Hill was especially difficult to travel in the winter months. Sometimes when my family tried to visit, we would have to back down the road and try again and again to make it up the last incline. This was even when dad had chains on the tires. Sometimes we made it, and sometimes we had to turn around and return home.

The snow may have hindered travel, but it never dampened our spirits. If we went home, my sisters and I would go outside and play with friends. We thought that the snow was beautiful and made just for us. Snowball fights, snow forts, and king of the hill were always fun entertainment.

◆◆◆

The pasture behind our grandparents' house was a wonderful place for us kids to sleigh ride and make snowmen. We would play for hours until our feet hurt from the cold. Then we would go in and warm our hands and feet by the fire. Afterward, we would go back out and do it all over again.

I remember a night when the snow was particularly deep, and our family, Thomas and Florence, and their family were stranded on Fuller Hill. The snow was too deep and crusty for my sisters, cousins, and me to ride our sleds because the sleds sank in the deep snow. This caused us to be departed from our sleds letting the crusty snow scrape our tender faces as we flew sledless down the hill.

Grandpa was always a creative and adventurous man. He came up with the idea that all of us kids would remember for all our lives. Grandpa asked us if we wanted to go on a snow-boat ride. We didn't know what he was talking about, but it sounded fun. We all jumped up and down, excited to see what escapade our grandfather had in mind.

Grandpa disappeared for a little while. Soon we heard the sound of his tractor coming toward us. Behind it was attached a flat-bottom boat. When he reached us, he told everyone to jump in. My sisters, cousins, dad, Uncle Don, Uncle Thomas, and I boarded the small boat. Dad and Thomas kept Linda and Mary close to them to keep them warm. The rest of us kids never felt the cold as we laughed and enjoyed the magical night of unmeasurable joy.

That night, Grandpa pulled our crew around and around the large field. We were both happy and in awe of the spectacularly beautiful star-filled night and sparkling snow. It was a true winter wonderland filled with memories that would last forever.

◆◆◆

It was Christmas time once again. Mom and Dad had purchased a magnificent Christmas gift for Grandma and Grandpa. Their special gift was a **swinger polaroid camera** that developed pictures within seconds of snapping the picture. They made all of us girls swear not to tell our grandparents what they bought.

One evening before Christmas, Grandpa teasingly asked my sisters and me what our family got him for Christmas. Chris unwittingly let the cat out of the bag.

Bless her heart; she was trying to keep her promise. She replied, "I can't tell you, but I will give you a hint. It takes pictures."

My mouth dropped open in shock, and Grandpa laughed hysterically, but Chris did not realize that she had told her Grandpa exactly what he was getting for Christmas.

♦♦♦

Deer season in the 1950s and 1960s was a big event in the Catskills, especially around the Corbett and Downsville areas. In Downsville, the Eagle Hotel hung its guest's trophy bucks from their second-story balcony. There was always a slew of them hanging there during deer season.

The local men often strapped their bucks to the hood of their vehicles and drove around town to show them off. I remember my dad saying wow, so and so got a big one as we went by their vehicle.

♦♦♦

It was common practice to visit trash dumps in the 1960s'. People often found very useful things at these sites. There is a saying, "One man's junk is another man's treasure." For instance, my grandparents' house clock came from the dump. It was a regal wooden shelf clock made by Seth Thomas

There was a dump a few miles above the Finkle home. It was a relatively clean place and easy to get around in.

It was there that cousin Tommy acquired a fantastic skill. He sought and found old bicycles and bicycle parts. He learned to piece parts together through trial and error and make his own bikes.

Across the brook from my grandparents was a dirt road that led down to the lower lake. This road was the perfect place to try out Tommy's new equipment. It was here that both families of Thompson kids learned to ride bicycles. Learning to ride bikes wasn't always easy, but after a few scraped knees and bruises, we became pros, or so we thought.

Thomas and Florence rented an apartment on Montgomery Avenue in Downsville. This was just a short distance from our home on Knox Avenue. Because we lived close, we were often allowed to visit.

Up the street from their house was a steep dirt road that veered off to the right of Montgomery Avenue. It was hot out, and all of us kids decided to take two of the bicycles Tommy had made and ride them down the steep dirt road. Chris and Tommy would be the first, and then they would trade-off with the others.

The bicycles were different than the ones everyone was used to riding. They were ten-speed bikes that had brakes on the handlebars. Before taking off on their daredevil stunt, Tommy warned Chris that the foot peddles did not work and that she must use the handlebar brakes.

The other kids and I cheered them on as they headed down the steep decline. Then everyone noticed they were going way too fast and yelled for them to brake. Both

Chris and Tommy were screaming but not slowing down. For some reason, neither appeared to be hitting the brakes. No one knew if it was from sheer panic and they were trying to use their foot brakes or the handle brakes just didn't work.

At the bottom of the road was a house. The other kids and I started running toward the bottom of the hill because we knew Tommy and Chris would surely die. I guess we thought we could save them, but before we could get to them, we heard a loud bang as both hit the house straight on. God must have been with them that day. Other than a bump on their heads, a few scrapes, and hurt egos, they were both okay.

Aunt Florence was angry with everyone. She lectured us about how Tommy and Chris could have been killed, and we all should have known better than to try a stunt like that, even if the brakes did work. She took the bicycles away and said nobody could ride them for a week and then only on their street.

◆◆◆

Downsville was a small community but a nice place to grow up. The local school had a huge playground that was open all year round. It had tennis courts, a soccer field, a baseball field, a basketball court, and an outside swimming pool.

Often Dad and his brothers would watch a men's baseball game on the weekend, and all of us kids would play on the playground.

Being within walking distance of the swimming pool was great. My sisters and I took swimming classes in the morning and swam all afternoon. However, the first week we got bad sunburns, but we soon healed, and everyone was okay for the rest of the summer. Our skin glowed with a dark suntan, and our hair became almost blonde from the chlorine in the water.

When we weren't at the schoolyard, we often walked up the road from where we lived. A short distance from our house, the landscape turned into farm country and made a very scenic walk.

Downsville also had an inside movie theater next to the covered bridge. My sisters, cousins, and I were occasionally allowed to walk to it. We especially liked Elvis Presley movies.

◆◆◆

I enjoyed the pool for a month, and then I had an opportunity for my first paying job. Thomas and Florence had bought a house and moved to Walton, and Florence found a job there. The only problem was she had no one to watch her children. She asked if I would be allowed to watch them for her.

I was only eleven but had watched my sisters often when our mother had to go someplace. In the 1960s' children were more responsible because of how they were raised.

Mom and I both agreed I would babysit. I would stay with my aunt and uncle during the week and come home on the weekends. Florence would pay me fifteen dollars a week. I quickly did the math in my head (four weeks times fifteen dollars was sixty dollars). That was a lot of money back then, especially for a kid.

Due to my age and lack of cooking experience, I was not allowed to use the stove. The kids lived on peanut butter and jelly sandwiches, occasionally switching out with bologna and mustard. Everyone was tired of these sandwiches by the end of the summer, especially Randy.

An incident that I will never forget is the day one of the kids accidentally locked my cousins and me out of the house. I came up with the idea of lifting one of them through the open bathroom window. The only problem was no one saw the wasp nest. All the kids, including me, received more than one sting, causing us to run screaming to the front of the house.

I knew I couldn't cry even though I badly wanted to. While contemplating what to do, I remembered my grandpa saying, *if you ever get stung, put mud on the bite. It will relieve the pain and draw out the stinger.*

That evening when Florence returned home, she found all the kids and me covered head to toe in mud. One can only imagine what she was thinking.

At the end of summer, Florence paid me for babysitting. I was excited and bought my first dress with my own money. It was pink with white lace. The lace had a thin black ribbon that weaved from my neck toward my waist. I was so very proud.

Chapter Seventeen

My Dad had become a sought-after man in his profession of drilling and blasting. He had received an offer for the foreman position over drilling and blasting on a road construction job in Dutchess County. He would now have a more steady income and be able to better support his family.

Dad and Mom informed my sisters and me that we would move to Hosner Mountain Road in Hopewell Junction, New York. Thomas and Florence also would be moving there. Neither of our families realized that we would not ever again live in Delaware County, but that is a story for another time.

My family moved our trailer, and Mom enrolled us all in school. I was excited about going to Van Wyck Junior High in Fishkill. It was bigger than my school in Downsville and only had seventh through ninth grades.

Not long after our move, I found a couple of babysitting jobs. It was reasonably easy money for a twelve-year-old girl. I made fifty cents an hour in my first job, but the other paid me seventy-five cents an hour. I also had a job helping a lady clean once a week for one dollar an hour. I was quite a young entrepreneur.

I learned to manage my money, save for the future, and still have money to spend. This was great for me as I was in the ideal shopping location. There were many shopping centers around Fishkill and Poughkeepsie. My parents still bought my necessities, but I could purchase extra clothing with my money. It made me feel good to be able to do so.

One thing that the girls and I found to be funny was that George Washington sure did get around. It seemed like everywhere we turned, a sign said, "**George Washington** slept here."

♦♦♦

I had just turned thirteen when my mom told us she was pregnant. Everyone was so excited, even Dad, who once again hoped for a boy.

It was fun to ride with Mom to her doctor appointments. All seemed well until one day when we came home from school, a neighbor met us. Mom had been taken to the doctor that day. Later she returned home but was on complete bed rest, hoping she would go full term.

Baby sister Suzanne, however, had different plans. She came into this world three months early. She only weighed three pounds and ten ounces, but she was a fighter, and after a month in the hospital, she would come home to four coddling sisters.

Mom was in the hospital for a few days. I remember my sisters and me thinking we were doing something big by baking her a cake and decorating it with cheerios to spell out, Welcome Home Mom.

When Suzie finally made it home, my sisters and I spoiled her rotten. We dressed her like a doll and curled her hair. Swinger polaroid cameras were popular then, so we often poised her for cute little pictures. She was quite the little camera ham.

Suzie was not old enough to remember much about Fuller Hill, but there are many pictures of Grandma holding her and some of her posing on the dining room table. One of my favorites is a picture of Suzie standing in front of Grandma's sink, holding a fish almost as big as her.

◆◆◆

After Suzie was born, my parents purchased a bigger trailer and moved it a few lots down from where we lived.

We still made bi-weekly visits to Fuller Hill. Chris and I often spent a couple of weeks at a time with our grandparents during the summer. We always looked forward to these visits. They were times we always treasured.

Chris and I still went to the barn with Grandma and Don in the morning and again in the evening while Grandpa watched the six o'clock news. Our grandmother still made the best pancakes in the world.

Sometimes Grandma and Don would take us for a short walk up the road or down the dirt road toward the lower lake. Don often let us tag along when he hunted for woodchucks or checked his trap line at the upper lake.

It was still fun to ride along with Grandpa as he rode up and down the hill after lawbreakers and game poachers.

My sister and I always enjoyed it when company came to visit or when we went to Andes to visit our Great Uncles and cousins.

Some nights, before our grandparents came to bed, Chris and I would recall our dreams from when we lived in Corbett. We were going to have a double wedding when we grew up. The church would be decorated with the apple blossoms that grew along the dirt road behind our old house in Corbett. They were so pretty in the spring. Chris would wear her favorite color, lavender, and I would wear blue.

We now had new dreams for when we grew up. We were going to buy our grandparents' farm and live there forever. Our dreams were good, but unforeseen things would happen to our homeplace, making it impossible for them to be fulfilled. But life would still be good for us, and we would witness some very historical events.

♦♦♦

The summer of 1969 was historically significant. It was the summer before my sophomore year, July 20, 1969. Dad was watching the TV when the **first moonwalk** took place. He shouted for my sisters and me to come in to watch. It will be forever etched in my mind.

It thrilled me to see Niel Armstrong wearing a spacesuit and bouncing from the lack of gravity on the moon. His words still sound in my ears, "That's one small step for man, one giant leap for mankind." These words encouraged me as a young girl. It made me realize that anything was possible if I set my mind to doing something,

♦♦♦

August 1969 brought a whole different type of history. The largest music festival ever held, "**Woodstock**," with big-name bands like *Creedence Clearwater Revival.*

My family lived next to the Taconic State Parkway. It was unbelievable the number of Hippies we saw that were hitchhiking with signs that said "Woodstock." My sisters and I were not allowed outdoors because our father said it was unsafe for young ladies to be outside.

Woodstock was held in Bethel, New York, which is in Sullivan County. This county borders Delaware County and is close to Fuller Hill.

I was not exaggerating the number of people hitchhiking. [9] *It was estimated that over four hundred thousand people attended the Woodstock Festival. So many that the event couldn't set up fences and booths to collect money, so they let everyone in for free. Sullivan County called a state of emergency. Many roads were closed.*

Drugs like LSD were prominent at this time in history. It is said that LSD and Marijuana were free-flowing during this concert.

Drugs were also a big problem with school-aged kids. Every time I turned around, it seemed that I heard of someone in my school who had overdosed. It was nothing to come to school and see someone tripping out and trying to climb a wall. If anyone attended a school function, they were told never to leave their soda can unattended.

♦♦♦

One of the projects my dad was very proud of was his part in building the **World Trade Center in New York City, New York**. After completing his road construction job, he became part of the crew that drilled out the basement of this magnificent building. He loved being a part of such a historical project. It is such a shame that it was destroyed in 2001 by foreign terrorists and is remembered as a sad and tragic day called nine-eleven.

♦♦♦

The school dress code in the 50s until the late 60s was girls wore dresses and boys wore nice slacks and button-up shirts. In the late 60s, the mini-skirt made its debut. Some girls wore really short mini-skirts and were made to go home and change. The Thompson girls did not go to this extreme but showed a little leg.

I attended John Jay High School in 1969 when the dress code changed. Girls were now allowed to wear pantsuits. Not necessarily business pantsuits, but nice dressy pantsuits.

♦♦♦

When I was in school, my sisters and I lived very sheltered and protected lives. I was allowed to go to one dance or basketball game monthly. This was one disadvantage of being the oldest. The rules are always stricter for the firstborn. However, these rules slacked a little for my sisters but not much.

When we left for an event, our father always gave us a dime to call home if we needed him. Only one time in high school did I use this dime, and that was because Chris and I became sick with German measles at a dance. But all my life until I married, I had that dime, and I was not afraid to use it if I had to.

Our father's protective arm would be there even after we graduated. This became obvious to me a few years later when I worked in the office on the same road construction project as my father. A young man I worked with asked me out, but he turned out not to be a gentleman, and I asked him to take me home, which he did, maybe because my dad's nickname at work was Mad Dog. No one messed with Mad Dog's daughters.

♦♦♦

[10] *1955-1973 America was involved in a war called the "**Vietnam War**. Many say it was not a war but a conflict, but either way, 58,220 U.S. military personnel lost their lives, and 1,626 are still missing in action.*

In the late 60s' heartbreaking films of battles were shown every night on the evening news. I remember the constant anxiety and sorrow this caused many families as they watched and worried about their loved ones.

Men eighteen and older had to register and were drafted into the war by what was called a lottery. Those drafted made up the majority of the military force. However, some young men dodged the draft and moved to Canada.

The men who served in this war were not given the honor they deserved when returning home. People blamed them for the war, but in reality, they had no say in this war. Many of these young men did not want to be there themselves but were drafted and had to comply. The ones who did enlist thought they were doing their patriotic duty but had no say in the battles of this war.

Epilogue

In 1970, before my Junior year of High School, my father was offered a promotion to Superintendent of drilling and blasting. With this new job, he would have guaranteed work all year, better wages, and financial security. Our family would be moving again, but this time, it would be over ten hours away to Flatwoods, West Virginia. The girls and I were excited but sad simultaneously because we knew we would not see as much of our grandparents or New York family.

Everyone felt at home in Braxton County, West Virginia, as we were still mountain people. We had moved to a State known as "The Mountain State."

My family's trailer was late in being moved, and we didn't get to move in it immediately. When we found out it hadn't arrived, we looked for a place to stay but could not find one (This area was not developed as it is now). To solve this temporary problem, we went to a local drive-in theater to kill time. Then we found a place nearby and spent the night in our Vista Cruiser Station wagon. It was miserable because Suzie cried all night long. The next night we were able to secure a chalet for a couple of days.

Our home finally arrived on my sixteenth birthday. Not everything was fully set up, but we still had cake and ice cream for Cindy's and my birthdays.

My sisters and I fell in love with West Virginia. We found the people to be very friendly. Everyone knew each other, and we were welcomed and even popular in school, unlike in the large schools we had attended. The only sad thing was that our family only got to visit our grandparents about once or twice a year due to the expense and length of time to return to Fuller Hill.

Shortly after our family settled in, Thomas and his family moved to Walkersville, WV. This was about half an hour from us. My sisters and I were excited to have family close by once again.

♦♦♦

Dad was hired as a consultant for Joy. They sought his expertise in drilling and blasting. He still held his regular job, but Joy often sent a plane to fly him to various places. Dad had a built-in math ability they sought. He could look at a job and know exactly what was required to drill and blast a cut.

The built-in-math ability that dad possessed became very evident years later when the law required blasters to be licensed. Because Dad went to work to help his mother support her family, he did not finish High School. This concerned him. Suzie helped him study by quizzing him. She would give Dad a geometry or trigonometry problem, and he would solve it in his head before she could type the problem into her Scientific calculator. Dad worried about this test but aced it. He was one of the most intelligent men I ever knew.

♦♦♦

Our family moved to Roanoke, WV, which was close to Thomas and his family. I Graduated from Lewis County High School in 1972. I was thrilled that my Grandparents, Uncle Don, Aunt Sharon, Uncle Jeff, and their family could attend, but I was sad when they left.

In 1972, Thomas, Florence, and their family moved to Hialeah, Florida, and their children finished school and married there.

We were also going to move to Florida. Dad had a job lined up, but when we went there, Dad said it was too flat and had no mountains to blow up, so we returned to West Virginia.

During Christmas of 1972, we moved to Valley Bend in Randolph County, West Virginia. Chris graduated in 1974, and Cindy in 1976.

My family made a weekend visit to Fuller Hill in the Summer of 1973. We did not know it would be our last stay on Fuller Hill. Our Grandparents and Don moved to

Downsville that Fall. We still visited them, but it was now in Downsville.

In 1976 my parents purchased a house nearby in Huttonsville, WV. They lived there happily until they passed away. My two younger sisters would complete their schooling there.

My sister Cindy married in 1976, I married in 1977, Chris married in 1978, and Linda married in 1980. Almost a wedding a year.

After marrying, my husband Kenny and I still visited my grandparents, and I called them every weekend. Over the next few years, Kenny and I became parents to two wonderful sons. My grandparents only got to see our oldest son Kevin before they passed away; however, Grandma did see pictures of Eric. They were so proud of all their grandchildren and great-grandchildren.

♦♦♦

Grandma used to say, "Don't cross your bridges until you come to them." Well, many bridges have been crossed since my childhood. My grandparents' home was burnt to the ground. The old barn was torn down along with all the outbuildings, including the Fuller Brook Schoolhouse (Grandpa's garage). The pastures are overgrown with trees. The rose bushes my sisters and I loved are no longer visible. The old bridge that crossed the brook to the lower lake road is replaced with a new bridge with fancy stone pillars. There are now houses on the hill behind the upper lake. The pasture across the brook still looks the same, but everything else has changed. It saddens my heart that our treasured home no longer exists as it was in my childhood.

After the death of my grandparents, my husband Kenny, our children, and I continued to visit and call my Uncle Don until he died in 2019. My Mother and Father, Aunt Florence and Uncle Thomas, and most of our family of that generation have also gone home to be with Jesus. I miss them all tremulously. They were my rock and an unending source of love, encouragement, and knowledge.

Now, all I have to remind me of Fuller Hill is the old wooden clock my grandparents rescued from the dump, my sisters and cousins, a few family pictures, and of course, the beautiful memories of my Catskill Mountain roots.

My childhood family home may have been physically destroyed, but it will never be forgotten as long as my sisters, cousins, and I remember the love of family. Our heritage will always run deep in our blood and be passed on to our families

Citations and Credits

[1] "The Corbett Bridge" sign. The Downsville Women's Club, Corbett, NY. Used by permission. (Viewed 08 August 2019).

[2, 3] Corbett and Gregorytown Brief History, Corbett and Gregorytown Brief History - Colchesterhistoricalsociety.org (google.com) Used by permission, (accessed December 29, 2022).

[4] Wikipedia contributors, "Pepacton Reservoir," *Wikipedia, The Free Encyclopedia,* https://en.wikipedia.org/w/index.php?title=Pepacton_Reservoir&oldid=1094648687 (accessed December 29, 2022).

[5] Colchester Historical Society – Tub Mills Driving Tour Sign. Used by permission.

[6] Wikipedia contributors, "Downsville Bridge," Wikipedia, The Free Encyclopedia, https://en.wikipedia.org/w/index.php?title=Downsville_Bridge&oldid=1112106066 (accessed December 27, 2022).

[7] Biographical Review - 1895 The Leading Citizens of Delaware County, NY This volume contains Biographical Sketches of The Leading Citizens of Delaware County New York Biography is the home aspect of history Boston Biographical Review Publishing Company 1895 Section

13 - pages 589 through 649   Online since 1996 - created and managed by Joyce Riedinger   https://dcnyhistory.org/books/brevie13.html Used by permission, (accessed January 8, 2023).

[8] Delaware County NY Genealogy History site   W. W. Munsell 1797-1880   The Town of Colchester   Electronic text by Mary Nielson, IL https://dcnyhistory.org/books/muncol.html   Used by permission, (accessed January 8, 2023).

[9] Wikipedia contributors, "Woodstock," *Wikipedia, The Free Encyclopedia,* https://en.wikipedia.org/w/index.php?title=Woodstock&oldid=1130122856 (accessed January 5, 2023).

[10] Wikipedia contributors, "Vietnam War," *Wikipedia, The Free Encyclopedia,* https://en.wikipedia.org/w/index.php?title=Vietnam_War&oldid=1131029377 (accessed January 2, 2023).

Made in the USA
Columbia, SC
27 May 2023

f2766d11-eeda-461d-a717-725b53fa97abR01